Hope in the Garden for All Seasons

90-DAY DEVOTIONAL

REBECCA CARPENTER

DEEP
WATERS
BOOKS

Hope in the Garden for All Seasons: 90-Day Devotional
Copyright © 2025 Rebecca Carpenter
Published by Deep Waters Books, P.O. Box 692301, Orlando, FL 32869
www.deepwatersbooks.com
Cover Design: June Hardee
Printed in the United States of America

ISBN: 978-1-956520-20-0 (Hardcover) | ISBN: 978-1-956520-19-4 (Paperback) | LCCN 2026900577

Publisher's Cataloging-in-Publication data
Names: Carpenter, Rebecca, author.
Title: Hope in the garden for all seasons / Rebecca Carpenter
Description: Orlando, FL: Deep Waters Books, 2022.
Identifiers: ISBN: 978-1-956520-19-4 (paperback) | 978-1-956520-20-0 (hardcover) | LCCN 2026900577
Subjects: LCSH Christianity--Prayers and devotions. | Grief--Religious aspects--Christianity. | Prayers. | Spiritual life--Christianity. | Christian life. | BISAC RELIGION / Christian Living / Devotional | RELIGION / Christian Living / Death, Grief, Bereavement
Classification: LCC BV245 .C37 2025 | DDC 242/.8--dc23

In this series of meditations and reflections, Rebecca shares her personal insights gained from experiencing both joys and challenges in daily living. Reading her personal stories can help us see more deeply that lessons can be learned in both the wilderness and the beautiful garden times in our lives.

She relates how our Divine Creator can open our eyes to his presence, walking with us in both joys, sorrows, and in all other challenges we may face. Knowing the promises and presence of the Lord provides her with an anchor that keeps her safe in all situations. May these meditations encourage you to find that safe anchor as well.

~ Dr. Larry Selig
Pastor and author: *Discovering Your Spiritual DNA,*
Prayers God Loves to Answer
Discovering the Counter-Cultural Jesus:
Insights from the Holy Land and Gospel of Mark
Oviedo, Florida

Rebecca Carpenter's latest book is a refreshing break from the chaos of our current world of confusion and disorder. Her everyday thoughts give way to daily devotionals that are like beautiful songs to God.

Rebecca takes us out of our reality, often into the surroundings of nature in her garden, to allow us to feel the serenity that helps us to be in a prayerful mindset. From the first to the last of Rebecca's ninety devotionals, I felt invited into and uplifted into her world of natural beauty, grace and faith. She encourages us to have hope even amidst our wildernesses. Rebecca's faith and servant's heart inspire one to be a better member of God's community and to remember God's promises of hope.

~ Maura McKay
Retired VP of Operations
Harland Financial Solutions
DeLand, Florida

Rebecca's book profoundly touched my heart; it healed my spirit. Her book felt personal, as if it was written for me; each devotional felt as if God Himself was delivering me from heartbreak and disappointments. This was a time in my life of dried bones and languishing hope, but Rebecca's unique soothing and loving writing style brought understanding, encouragement, solace, joy, wisdom, peace, and healing in a season when I needed it the most. I, too, was trying to find hope in my own garden, but it wasn't until I started to read this book that I felt a gush of living waters running through my soul. It was that redemption and restoration that lifted me up with a renewed sense of hope.

I am confident that every reader will experience this downpour of God's love over their lives through this anointed and gifted writer, who touches hearts and soothes the spirit within.

~ Gretchka Saliceti-Herrera
Fitness Instructor and Aspiring Author
DeLand, Florida

Each page of this book weaves truth through vibrant storytelling.

My grandma writes lessons she's learned from her personal experiences with God. She invites readers into the joy and peace that come from walking with the Lord. Every story will draw you in more, until you feel as if you yourself are sitting on her porch, deep in conversation, learning from the wisdom she has to share.

~ Emily Storms
College Student
Writer: *Sisterhood Blog*
Winter Springs, Florida

Dedication

To my amazing granddaughters
who love Jesus and
are making a difference
in the lives of others.

Day 1: My Charming Retreat

Place your trust in the Eternal; rely on Him completely;
never depend on your own ideas and inventions.
Give Him the credit for everything you accomplish,
and he will smooth out and straighten the road that lies ahead.
Proverbs 3:5–6 VOICE

After months of staying inside, I ventured out to my patio for a predawn devotional time. Bronchitis and allergies had kept me from enjoying the beauty and solitude of the lake for weeks.

In the crisp morning air, the enchanting view welcomed me back. A half-moon glowed in the inky sky. Lunar light beamed as the sun gently overtook the darkness. Tweets, trills, and melodies formed a chorus of hidden singers.

Swirling mist performed a ballet above the shadowy water. Dragonflies twirled above the lakeside plants. Dewdrops twinkled on emerald grass. A filmy scarf of pale green adorned bald cypress trees as they emerged from their winter sleep. Pink, yellow, and orange blooms decorated the plants that had survived the winter freezes.

"

My extended time indoors had allowed only glimpses of the lake through windows, so the incredible scene mesmerized me. Everything appeared new and exciting. Light rain had washed away some of the yellow dusting of pollen, and I could return to my favorite patio chair. However, as I lingered to savor the splendor of the dawn, coughing returned. Unfortunately, allergy season remained.

Although I longed to stay outside in my charming retreat, wisdom whispered to leave. Continued exposure to the pesky plant allergens would again trigger an attack on my body.

A decision had to be made. I could pretend to feel good and linger in an unhealthy environment, or I could sensibly avoid triggers that might cause harm.

Each day, we have choices to make. Sometimes between good and bad. Frequently between good and better, or even good and best. Immediate desires may lead to decisions that can have undesirable consequences.

As I prepared to go into the house, a cardinal chirped at me. His scarlet feathers glistened as he bid me farewell—a perfect ending to my visit and a reminder that eventually I would be able to return to my porch.

Loving Father, thank you for creation that speaks to us. Give us wisdom to make the best possible decisions each day.
Amen.

Day 2: Flower Blessing for a Widow

*The one who listens to me, who carefully seeks me in
everyday things and delays action until my way is
apparent, that one will find true happiness.*
Proverbs 8:34 VOICE

While strolling through the store, I purchased flowers to create bouquets for two friends. One faced surgery, and the other had COVID. Later in the day, I left the colorful blooms at their front doors with a short devotional.

That evening, I sent a text to a friend whose husband had been enduring cancer treatment and ended up in the hospital after a fall. She replied that he wasn't doing well.

The following day, the Holy Spirit nudged me to buy more flowers on my way home. After a tiring day, the blooms went into a vase on the counter while I rested on the couch.

On my way to volunteer the next morning, I left a bouquet for the lady whose husband had cancer. Instead of calling, I sent her a text to look outside her front door.

"}

Her quick answer surprised me. "Oh my gosh, how did you know? The flowers are beautiful. My husband died last night. Thank you so much."

I had no idea her husband was so sick and near death. However, Jesus knew she needed a special reminder that she was loved and not alone.

After I told her God prompted me to buy flowers for her, she replied, "I knew it. How powerful is that?"

Because I listened and obeyed the prodding of the Holy Spirit instead of ignoring it, the Lord blessed us both.

*Loving Father, thank you for nudging us
to listen and be a small part
of blessing others.
Amen.*

Day 3: Waddle or Swim

For you created my inmost being;
you knit me together in my mother's womb.
I praise you because I am fearfully and wonderfully made;
your works are wonderful, I know that full well.
Psalm 139:13–14

Movement caught my eye. A pair of mallard ducks waddled from the lake onto my lawn. They traveled through one flower bed and into another.

They stopped in the grass. Their heads swiveled in unison, one way and then the next. Tail feathers wiggled while the rest of their small bodies remained still. Stubby, orange legs, almost hidden in the grass, propelled them.

I often observed them form a tiny wake on the mirrored lake as they gracefully glided from shore to shore. They rarely visited my yard. Never had I seen them so close to my house.

I tiptoed to the screen for a better look. The nondescript female led the brightly colored male as they left. A few minutes later, they reappeared from the opposite side of my home.

They didn't search for tasty morsels in the grass; instead, they waddled back and forth before they returned to the lake.

In the water, they swim artistically and easily because God created them for swimming. However, they awkwardly totter on land with their stubby legs and webbed feet. No matter how they might try, the ducks will never walk elegantly like an egret or soar like an eagle. They won't sing like a meadowlark or catch fish like a heron.

Likewise, we need to embrace the gifts and talents God has given us and follow his path for us. We shouldn't try to soar like an eagle if we are a duck. God made us as we are to use us exactly as he planned.

Creator, thank you for making us unique with a special plan.
Help us accept our gifts and talents so we don't strive to be
like someone else. Guide us each day
in the way we should go.
Amen.

Day 4: Reflecting Lights

When Jesus spoke again to the people, he said,
"I am the light of the world. Whoever follows me
will never walk in darkness, but
will have the light of life."
John 8:12

Clouds hung low over the horizon. Waves emerged from the haze and rolled to the shore. A sprinkling of cars drove over the packed sand and parked above the water's edge.

Below the balcony, Smyrna Dunes Park stretched from the grass of the condo complex to the end of the peninsula. Visitors experienced nature without damaging it as they strolled the boardwalks through the dense forest and to the beach. In the distance, a lengthy rock jetty jutted into the ocean, its endpoint disappearing into the mist.

Across the inlet, the historic New Smyrna Lighthouse stood as a sentinel of the past. Built in 1835, the structure's brilliant light saved sailors from crashing onto the dangerous shore. The gigantic light blinks in the darkness no longer as protection but as a tribute to bygone days.

Clouds glowed as the sun rose above the horizon. A break in the gray curtain revealed a slice of the golden sphere. Only a hint of sunrise painted the sky.

Clusters of miniature people walked along the almost deserted beach. Surfers waited in the rolling waves to catch the best one. Their dark heads looked like birds huddled on the ocean. From the eighth-floor balcony, everything appeared tiny.

From my perspective, I saw teeny people moving through the park, on the beach, and in the water. But I couldn't hear their conversations, see their faces, or perceive their thoughts.

My attention shifted from visitors to the two bright lights. The lighthouse glowed to my left, and the sun shone to my right. For years, the beacon stood as a safeguard for sailors. Now it is a focal point and a reminder of its past glory. The sun rises every day, providing continuous light and warmth even when obscured by heavy clouds.

God's faithfulness endures like the sun he created. He looks down on the world from the heights. Instead of seeing only tiny figures, he peers into our hearts to see our pain and joys.

The light of Jesus shines so we can reflect it to the world. His light isn't an obsolete beacon like the lighthouse. Nor is it hidden behind the clouds like the sun. His Spirit lives in us when we accept him, and then we can shine brightly with his love in a dark world.

Loving Father, when we feel alone and discouraged, we know you are faithful to love and protect us. Show us how we can shine your light as a beacon for those around us.
Amen.

Day 5: The Three-Week Gift

*Rejoice always, pray without ceasing, in everything give thanks
for this is God's will for you in Christ Jesus.*
1 Thessalonians 5:16–18

Stuck on the couch for three weeks with coughing and fatigue. Missing special activities. Sleepless nights. All of this altered my holiday plans.

However, as I read Paul's command to "Rejoice always, pray without ceasing, in everything give thanks" (1 Thessalonians 5:16–18), a different purpose unfolded. Looking back on the frustration of my extended isolation, I understood that God would use my trials for good.

While I snuggled on my couch, a pile of books kept me company. One after another, I devoured them as important messages filled my head. A few were feel-good novels that I rapidly read. But most delved into important matters and touched my heart.

A friend's book, *Where No Roads Go* by Carin LeRoy, transported me to the jungles of Papua New Guinea, where she and her family ministered for thirteen years. The constant struggles they faced made my temporary illness seem insignificant. I thought of missionaries around the world who face dangers, loneliness, and heartbreak as they follow God's calling.

Then I read *A Stubborn Hope* by Jeanne DeTellis, who served for many years with her family in Haiti. Extreme challenges faced them, but they also felt the call of God for the impoverished citizens of that country.

Wurmbrand: Tortured for Christ: The Complete Story by Richard Wurmbrand graphically detailed the horrors he and his wife faced during years of imprisonment. They never renounced their faith but continued to share the gospel and began Voice of the Martyrs, which continues even today to assist persecuted Christians around the world.

Each additional book I read about oppressed Christians helped me see the agony they faced, but also the joy in following God's plan. Some of them escaped, but thousands have been martyred for their faith.

My daily devotional time lengthened as I hungered for more of the Bible and prayed more often. With fewer distractions, I listened to the Holy Spirit more intently.

I realized I had been on a three-week spiritual retreat. What a gift!

As I reflected on what I learned and experienced, I prayed for more boldness in my faith and to become more like Jesus.

Loving Father, thank you for slowing us down so we can know you better. Show us daily your plan and what we are to do.
Amen.

Day 6: Thankful for the Rain

Open your mouths with thanks!
Sing praises to the Eternal.
Strum the harp in unending praise to our God.
Who blankets the heavens with clouds, sends rain to water
the thirsty earth, and pulls up each blade of grass
upon the mountainside.
Psalm 147:7–8 VOICE

Heavy clouds hovered overhead and cast gloom over the lake. From my patio, I noticed a hummingbird return, after many days, to nearly barren plants. His thin beak dipped into the two remaining blooms.

Normal summer showers bypassed my area for weeks. When rain droplets dotted the glassy lake, I stopped reading and cherished the long-awaited shower. The life-giving rain enhanced my devotional time on the patio. Random drops created circles all over the lake. Sheets of rain brought a deluge from the opposite shore to my yard. Breezes tossed watery beads onto the screen where they clung tightly and waited for the sparkle of sunshine.

Drips hit the gutter like Morse code of a telegraph message. With eyes closed, I listened to a symphony of water sounds. A crescendo and decrescendo of rain came as though a conductor raised and lowered his baton. Tiny drops added gentle percussion.

During a seasonal rain, I probably would have stayed inside the house and not noticed the nuances of the storm. Perhaps I would have even complained about the disruption in outside activities. However, the end of the drought brought thankfulness and joy while I watched the refreshment of my yard. It reminded me of God's provision and faithfulness for us too. He knows and supplies our needs.

Complicated lives bring periods of sadness, uncertainty, and despair. Likewise, we delight in times of joy, peace, and hope when we depend on Jesus.

Like a child who forgets to say thank you, we often neglect to show gratitude to our Creator for our blessings.

King Jesus, thank you for rain and sunshine,
along with times of tranquility and trials.
Each one teaches and brings us closer to you.
Amen.

Day 7: Cloudy Eyes

*So from now on we regard no one from a worldly point of view.
Though we once regarded Christ in this way, we do so no
longer. Therefore, if anyone is in Christ, the new creation has
come. The old has gone, the new is here!*
2 Corinthians 5:16–17

A wall of fog concealed the lake. Bit by bit, drabness dispersed to reveal the nearby shoreline. However, a veil of haze formed a fuzzy view of the lake.

Before eye surgery, cloudy lenses distorted my eyesight. Because cataracts developed over time, I had no idea my vision was flawed. Finally, when reading glasses didn't help me see text better and distant views appeared blurry, I realized there was a problem. An eye exam confirmed it was time to remove the cataracts.

After my first surgery, the bathroom light glowed like a beacon. Kitchen lights blazed with new intensity. Car headlights beamed like spotlights. With my corrected eye, white shirts glistened. They appeared dull beige with my other eye. I opened and closed one eye at a time to experience the contrast in colors and brilliance.

I had friends perform my simple eye test by looking at my white water bottle with one eye at a time. Several saw it as beige instead of pure white. Like me, they didn't realize their color vision was skewed.

For years, cloudiness affected my vision without me recognizing it. Only after the removal of the imperfections did I truly understand the defects I learned to live with.

Every person sees the world through their own unique lens, which may be distorted due to their life situations. We may not notice our perspective is clouded until the imperfections are removed.

In Jesus, we are new creations with the veil slipped off.

Father, thank you for giving us new life
and helping us see life through your eyes.
Amen.

Day 8: Healing Tears

Shadowy figures blended into an immense blur. With one cataract removed, I expected clear vision in my left eye, like I had after I had LASIK surgery years earlier. However, I couldn't read or work on my computer with blurry vision.

Watching TV wasn't easy either. When I tried to close my fuzzy eye, my eyelid kept popping open. Finally, I positioned myself on the couch with a pillow holding my eye shut. That worked—I could watch a detective program with my distance eye. The cozy pose lulled me to sleep. I missed the end of the show.

When the fuzziness didn't improve, I discovered side effects of the surgery could last for days or weeks. I texted friends to see how they fared, but most didn't remember.

I trudged off to bed. With tape across half of my face to hold the shield in place and my sleep apnea device in my mouth, I laughed at my peculiar image staring back at me in the mirror.

Way before dawn, I awoke and wondered if my sight had improved. But my left eye refused to open. Scenarios swirled. Had the eye drops acted like glue? Perhaps an infection?

Reluctantly, I shuffled to the bathroom to assess the problem. My eye opened in slow motion when I removed the shield. Since the doctor's instructions said not to get the eye wet or touch it for a week, I carefully wiped off the gooey discharge.

Minutes later, I began my morning devotions wearing reading glasses and still not seeing clearly. Instantly, a multitude of tears washed over my eyes. Grief poured out for my husband's passing.

Hope of better vision. Thankfulness for prayers. Sadness at being lonely. Gratitude for caring friends. Anxiety about not knowing if my vision would improve. Peace from God for all I faced.

More tears and emotions spilled out. As they slowed, I looked down at the Bible and sang praises. Without glasses, I saw clearly for the first time in years.

The Lord used tears to cleanse my eyes and heart.

Loving Father, thank you for being close to us when
we are sad, lonely, thankful, anxious, or peaceful.
You can take what seems difficult and make it into
something priceless.
Amen.

Day 9: How to Be a Reflection

You are the light of the world.
A town built on a hill cannot be hidden.
Neither do people light a lamp and put it under a bowl.
Instead they put it on its stand, and it gives light to
everyone in the house. In the same way, let your light
shine before others, that they may see your good
deeds and glorify your Father in heaven.
Matthew 5:14–16

Total darkness shrouded the world beyond my patio. A solitary lamp illuminated the pages of my Bible and devotionals.

When I glanced toward the lake, a sliver of moon hung behind the trees. Its light pierced the darkness. My eyes focused on the bright crescent. The unusual occurrence drew me away from reading my Bible for a few minutes to study the sky.

The moon played hide and seek behind the trees and within moments almost disappeared out of sight behind the limbs. Then a spotlight from the rising sun brightened the heavenly body.

Gradually, a rosy hue formed a background behind the forest as the sun rose higher. Night retired, and a new day began.

The moon's radiance does not originate from within; it is simply reflected light from the sun. During a lunar eclipse, the moon appears dark as it blocks out the solar rays.

Like the moon, on our own, we glow dimly in the shadowy world. However, when we follow Jesus and his teachings, he changes our lives. We reflect his light into the dark world with our love, kindness, and compassion.

Our homes, schools, workplaces, and to the ends of the earth, people are searching for hope, love, and a purpose for their lives. As Christians, we can proclaim Jesus as the source of our faith, peace, and contentment.

Loving Father, as we ponder the life of Jesus,
help us be more like him.
Guide us each day as we shine his light
for those in darkness.
Amen.

Day 10: "My Gosh!"

O h my gosh! Oh my gosh!" I kept talking aloud to myself.

Before dawn, I had sat on my patio reading devotional books and my Bible. As the sun rose, a dim lake emerged along with shadowy trees on the shore. My eyes swept the landscape a few times as darkness disappeared, but I kept reading and ignored my surroundings.

When I finally looked up, an indistinct shape blotted out the plants near the cypress trees. Then a large dark creature turned toward the patio, probably because of my light. He looked intently at me. I stared back. For a few moments, we stood like statues. I wanted to grab my phone to take a picture, but I had forgotten to bring it outside with me. I kept repeating, "Oh my gosh!"

When the adolescent black bear got tired of gazing at me, he loped off toward my neighbor's house. I walked outside to

"

see where he went, but also kept glancing back behind me to make sure no mama or papa bear trailed him. When I couldn't see him anymore from my windows, I returned to my patio.

At our previous house, we saw bears rather frequently. At this home, I only observed a large bear across the lake once several years ago. Never a few feet from me.

The wonder of God's creation filled me with awe. From microscopic to mammoth, he created plants and animals of all kinds. If I had not looked up at that precise moment, I would have missed an opportunity to see a bear closely. How many times have I not noticed God's other marvelous gifts?

Superfluous distractions may prevent me from experiencing miracles and blessings. When I take time to observe, I have discovered glistening spider webs, sparkles on the lake, and a glorious cloud-filled sky. The Holy Spirit has prompted me to look up to see a Monarch butterfly, a deer across the lake, and the dancing of a child.

Stop, breathe, and take in God's glory so we can exclaim, "Oh my gosh!"

Father, help us take time to notice wonderful
moments and opportunities that come into our lives.
Don't let us be distracted by things that don't matter.
Amen.

Day 11: A Protective Cage

I have told you these things,
so that in me you may have peace.
In this world you will have trouble.
But take heart! I have overcome the world.
John 16:33

When my town became a Monarch city, I decided to get involved and help the colorful insects. I dutifully prepared three butterfly cages. The time-consuming but rewarding endeavor brings joy when butterflies are released and soar with the wind.

Green, white, and black–striped caterpillars crawled up bare stems. I kept busy each day by cleaning the cages to prevent diseases and supplying fresh food to these voracious eaters. When I collected milkweed leaves for my soon-to-be butterflies, I searched every one for teeny white eggs and miniature caterpillars. With many predators such as wasps, bees, and lizards, the population of butterflies in the area had dwindled.

In my cages, these little creatures experienced protection and nourishment. Within a few weeks, I watched them transform from rice-sized eggs to magnificent adults as they progressed through metamorphosis. Although a perfect arrangement for a while, they couldn't live permanently in my confined spaces. They needed to spread their wings and fly outside.

In our uncertain, often scary world, we also might be tempted to stay inside: secluded, sheltered, and away from disasters. Even though God protects and guides us when we become Christians, we are not promised an easy life. The Bible instructs and leads us in the way we should go. Biblical teaching and fellowship with other Christians give us peace, hope, and strength for our journey.

Jesus never promised us a trial-free life, but did promise he would never leave us. With him as our protector, we can soar and make a difference in the world around us.

Loving Father, we don't know your plan
but trust you to teach and lead us.
Amen.

Day 12: Distressed Butterflies

You must speak my words to them, whether they listen
or fail to listen, for they are rebellious.
Ezekiel 2:7

Four chrysalises opened. From the top of my butterfly cage, two butterflies hung like lovely ornaments. They flapped wings and yearned to take off. Unfortunately, the other two insects landed upside-down on the bottom of the enclosure. Thread-sized legs grasped frantically at the air. They couldn't fly or even turn themselves over.

When I unzipped the cage, the active ones crawled onto my hand before flying away. The remaining ones needed help. Each one tried to clutch my finger but dropped to the cage floor. Over and over, they attempted to hold on. Finally, the delicate creatures clung to me as I pulled my hand out of the enclosure. However, with little strength, they soon tumbled to the ground.

Time after time, I put a twig near their teeny legs and laid them on the nearby milkweed plants. They squeezed valiantly but plummeted. Finally, both hung from the leaves while fluid filled their wings.

I checked on them every few minutes. Thankfully, after a couple of hours, one flapped its wings and zoomed off. However, the second butterfly's wings refused to open completely. No matter how many times I tried to rescue it, the wee creature couldn't fly.

For an unseen reason, God's plan never came to fruition for this one. I felt a twinge of sadness in my heart at losing the little one. But I rejoiced a few weeks later when twenty-eight butterflies flew away from my protection.

God doesn't want any to perish. Butterflies or people.

Often, we nurture and guide those who falter. We might try over and over to help them know Jesus. Many believe, but some don't. I won't give up on my butterflies even though a few don't survive. Likewise, we shouldn't stop sharing the love of Jesus even though some people reject him. We can let the Holy Spirit lead us and leave the results to God.

Creator, the beauty of your creation captivates us.
But even amid the beauty, there is sadness, grief,
and rejection. Guide us to help those who soar
and those who falter.
Amen.

Day 13: The Open Door

For months, I became an expert at maintaining three butterfly cages. Eighty-three monarchs hatched successfully! The time-consuming chore brought rewards when butterflies took off to flitter around the yard.

One day, I found two chrysalises hanging from the top of a cage when I cleaned it. A couple of days later, I noticed that I hadn't zipped up the flap on the habitat completely. I wasn't concerned until I saw empty chrysalises. No butterflies dangled from the mesh.

My eyes roamed my enclosed patio and stopped at the far end near the ceiling. A monarch clutched the screen above my reach. I tried to entice the newly hatched butterfly to latch onto a broom. She did for a couple of seconds and then moved higher. With an alluring flower stuck to the broom, I tried again. No success.

Even though she was far from the screen door, I left it open and hoped she would escape to the outside world. If she got out of a tiny opening in the cage, surely she could fly out of a big door. Hourly, I checked to see if she had flown away but she hadn't. I tried the broom again, but she ignored it.

For months, I cleaned cages, supplied milkweed, brought teeny eggs inside and released full-grown monarchs. My efforts protected these beautiful creatures from predators and ensured a safe environment, until I once forgot to zip the opening. The screen enclosure protected the Monarch from wind, rain, and most predators. But there were no blooms to feed her. She could see the world through the screen, but couldn't figure out how to escape to access it. She refused my attempts to rescue her.

Like my stubborn butterfly, we can also become entangled in difficult situations, perhaps caught in poor choices, addictions, and worldly vices. When God tries to show us a way out, we may run further away and refuse guidance. Enduring the familiar can trap us in unhealthy or dangerous situations.

God loves us and wants the best for his children. He leaves his door open so we can enter and have an abundant life with him.

Loving Father, you love us and want what is best for us.
But we must listen and move through your door
as you guide us.
Amen.

Day 14:
Disoriented Insects

*"Woe to the obstinate children," declares the L*ORD*,*
"to those who carry out plans that are not mine,
forming an alliance,
but not by my Spirit,
heaping sin upon sin.
Isaiah 30:1

Every few hours for the next several days, I searched for that stubborn butterfly that escaped from the cage and refused to leave my screened-in patio. I kept hoping she would fly through the open door to the outside.

Unfortunately, she remained at the top of the screen, almost at the ceiling. Each time I attempted to reach her, she would flap her wings like an out-of-control fan.

Other invaders entered through the wide-open door and joined her at the end of my patio. A huge dragonfly buzzed as it tried to propel itself through the screen. A wasp whizzed near me. My trusty broom tried to move the parade of insects toward the door.

The butterfly moved higher out of my reach. The dragonfly continued buzzing like a miniature saw. I dreaded the wasp that could cause me pain and swelling. All resisted my assistance for their freedom.

With a fly swatter in hand, I eliminated a wasp. Repeatedly, I tried to maneuver the remaining ones to the outside. Then a second dragonfly dive-bombed me from out of nowhere. He grabbed hold of the screen as I contemplated my dilemma.

Should the door remain open as a means of escape for the critters, or should it be closed to prevent more unwelcome intruders?

As I pondered the situation, the butterfly descended within my reach. She folded her tiny wings so I could gently grasp them. I hurried outside before I dropped her. She danced in the wind after the release.

When the butterfly fled her safe cage, she became disoriented and lost. Then intruders joined and added to the confusion. They all gathered close, but with no leader they floundered.

At times, we might be lost, confused, and trapped in complicated circumstances with no obvious escape. Jesus is a rescuer who has a perfect plan. He doesn't force us but desires that we obediently follow him.

Father, when we think we have all the answers but are in a mess,
show us how to follow your plan instead of our own.
Amen.

Day 15: How to Be a Poor Witness

My dear brothers and sisters,
take note of this:
Everyone should be quick to listen, slow to speak and
slow to become angry, because human anger does
not produce the righteousness
that God desires.
James 1:19–20

After lunch with friends in our quiet, quaint town, we heard shouting as we walked to our cars. We froze and gaped at the source of the unexpected outrage. Shoppers on both sides of the street stared at the spectacle.

A few feet from us, two trucks stopped traffic on the main thoroughfare. Both drivers stood beside their vehicles with doors open. The man at the back screamed curses and threatened the person he thought had offended him. From his escalating tirade, it was obvious that he believed the other motorist had intentionally driven in a way that was harmful to him. With so many recent shootings, I was afraid we were going to witness another road-rage casualty.

Thankfully, the first driver remained calm and didn't provoke his out-of-control opponent in the disturbing situation. He simply got into his truck and left.

When the first motorist took off, I hoped the irate man wouldn't follow and continue his outburst. As the crowd dispersed, I noticed a bumper sticker on the back of his truck from a local Christian radio station. Did he attach it to show his connection to their mission, or did someone else? In either case, his outburst produced a terrible Christian witness.

An instant burst of anger, a bit of gossip, laying on the horn at a slow driver, or a snide remark can ruin a witness to those who might already have a distorted view of Christians. If we wear a cross, attend church, or carry a Bible, people assume we are Christians, and some people may be happy to see us falter.

The incident reminded me that our actions don't have to be as outrageous as the furious driver's, but they can be just as damaging if we taint the world's view of Christianity.

Father, show us how to live like Jesus in our broken
world. Help us be kind and compassionate, even
when it's not easy and we don't want to.
Amen.

Day 16: The Tattered Sock

I tell you that this man, rather than the other,
went home justified before God. For all those who
exalt themselves will be humbled, and those who
humble themselves will be exalted.
Luke 18:14

I distinctly remember preparing for a friend's birthday party many decades ago. I selected a special dress and looked forward to seeing my third-grade friends.

We played Pin the Tail on the Donkey, dropped clothespins into an empty glass milk bottle, and everyone enjoyed cake and ice cream. Memories of who attended, what we ate, and presents received by the birthday girl have now dissolved over time. However, one game remains firmly planted in my mind. The details linger as though it happened yesterday.

The birthday girl's mom explained the unfamiliar game to us: "Everyone, form a circle, take off your right shoe, and place it in the middle. Music will play, and when it stops, grab your shoe and put it on. The last person to do that will be out. The remaining girls will continue when the music starts. The game will be over when only one girl is left."

The game sounded enjoyable to the rest of the group, but not to me. Immediately, everyone but me pulled off their shoes and formed a pile in the middle of the group.

My shoe stuck to my foot like glue. Horrors swirled in my young brain. I could toss in my left shoe and pretend I didn't know which shoe was the right one. My stomach could hurt so I could sit the game out. But then I wouldn't be able to have cake and ice cream.

After putting on a colorful dress that day, I'd selected a pair of white socks. One had a slight rip in the heel, which formed a huge hole when I yanked it on. Instead of finding another sock, for some strange reason, I used a diaper-sized safety pin to hold the gap together. Would the party stop when my huge safety pin revealed itself? Perhaps the group would think my parents couldn't afford decent socks.

Over the years, other situations triggered a similar feeling of self-consciousness. But as difficult as they have been, I survived. Now I can laugh about many of them, and even have fun sharing a few.

Vulnerability often enables folks to share their own shabby stories. Storytelling, especially of hard situations, can bring us together and help us heal the hurts.

Father, remind us that you love us even when we
mess up and feel tattered. Help us not to take
ourselves too seriously, and to depend on you
for getting us through.
Amen.

Day 17: Fall from the Tree

Now may the Lord of peace
himself give you peace at all times
and in every way.
The Lord be with all of you.
2 Thessalonians 3:16

Years ago, cars pulled into our gravel driveway for a family dinner. Aunts, uncles, and cousins filled our small, country home in Indiana.

My dad's large family held monthly dinners throughout my childhood, which brought us close together with happy times. However, that fall day included unpleasant memories for me. After a meal with tables of homemade delights, the cousins hurried outside to play. At that time, there were nine boys and four girls.

Someone suggested a game of Keep Away. With the odds against us girls, I whispered a plan to my cousin on how we could triumph over the guys. I climbed a tree and perched on one of the limbs. When we took the ball, I would reach down to grab it. A perfect idea that went wrong.

As I perched in the tree waiting for my moment, my slick sandal soles slipped on a branch, and I landed on my back on the ground. Faces stared down at me. My body hurt. Suddenly, adults surrounded me. Then I heard, "Look at her arm."

Over time, details became less clear, but a few unmistakable incidents remain. Someone scooped me up and placed me in the backseat of my uncle's car. I remember stopping at the local doctor's office. He gave me a shot and told my parents to take me to a hospital several miles away.

My dad sat with me while the x-ray machine hummed. When the technician moved my deformed arm to get a better image, intense pain filled me. Finally, after a series of pictures, the doctor pushed both bones into place. Never had I experienced so much agony. My parents had lovingly cared for me all my life with no serious medical issues or problems —until that day, when they couldn't take away my pain.

After a long, grueling afternoon, a hard plaster cast covered my arm, and we returned home. What began as a wonderful day ended with anguish and a changed life. No school for a week. No running around the playground at recess. No dance lessons.

That experience showed me the love of my parents and extended family. Even though I experienced such horrible pain, I survived and learned that pain is temporary. Our life experiences, both good and bad, continue to shape us.

*Father, even as children, we learn to trust you and
see you in those around us. Thank you for loving
families and helpful doctors.
Amen.*

Day 18: God's Guidance

Nevertheless, I am continually with You:
You hold me by my right hand.
You guide me with Your counsel and afterward receive me to glory.
Whom have I in heaven but You?
And there is none upon earth that I desire besides You.
My flesh and my heart fail; but God is the strength of my heart and
my portion forever.
Psalm 73:23–26 NKJV

A curtain of black covered my patio. A variety of sounds pierced the blackness. Crickets hummed their tune. The light from a small plane glowed and then slowly disappeared. Leaves on the trees rustled in the breeze.

Although I saw nothing beyond my lanai, I listened intently. Did I hear raindrops pattering on my roof, or was it an animal scurrying over the shingles? Perhaps a squirrel scampered from the oak tree's limbs or maybe a bear battered the branches? Because of the darkness, I wasn't totally sure.

As night turned to day, light illuminated the sky and peeked through the forest. Trees swayed with the wind. Another aircraft's lights twinkled in the emerging sky. Birds flew high and zoomed across the lake. In the light, I could see what was beyond my patio.

How often am I so engrossed in social media posts and computer stories that I don't research to determine whether they are true or not? Do I funnel everything I hear or read through a biblical lens? Does my imagination rule instead of listening to what God says?

When we read the Bible and pray regularly, our minds and hearts are more open to how God is working in our lives. Away from the constant sounds of technology, never-ending music, and blaring televisions, the nudge from the Holy Spirit becomes more apparent. His Word instructs us in how we should live.

Loving, patient Father, guide us as we learn to listen for your instructions. Help us obey you each day.
Amen.

Day 19: A Spot of Color in the Gloom

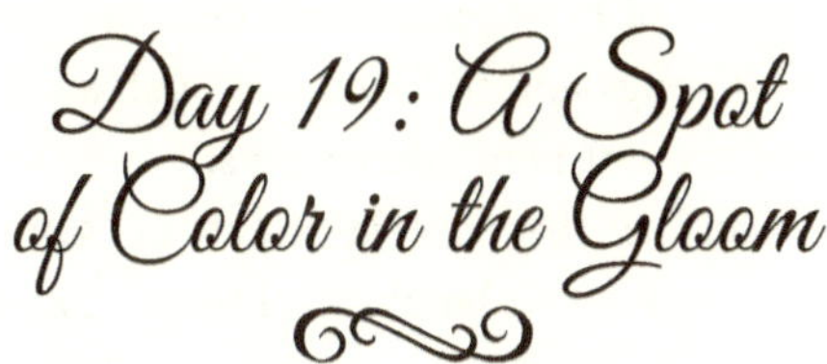

Let us not become weary in doing good,
for at the proper time we will reap a harvest
if we do not give up. Therefore, as we have
opportunity, let us do good to all,
especially to those who are of the household of faith.
Galatians 6:10 NKJV

An ashen blanket hovered over the lake, blotting out the sunrise. Morning light eased into the gloom. Somber trees cast their shadowy reflections onto the lake like a giant mirror. Naked cypress trees waited to be dressed by shoots of green. Winter's brown grass bordered the shoreline. Even vibrant green plants dimmed under slate clouds. Brown and gray birds flew among the trees and rustled leaves. A chorus of bird melodies filled the air from one end of the lake to the other. But a lone sandhill crane's harsh bellowing interrupted their happy songs.

Nothing about my view projected joy or excitement, yet a sense of peace and serenity wrapped me in a cozy shawl. An unexpected spot of color caught my attention. An azalea's pink blooms broke through the dreariness. I smiled. Despite its dismal surroundings, the breathtaking flower glowed and blessed me.

Even when our days bring discouragement and trials, we can find glimmers of hope, encouragement, and joy in nature around us. Bird songs and fluffy clouds push away doldrums. Gardens ignite contentment and dreams.

We can also be that special light in someone else's darkness. A smile or laughter brings happiness. An unanticipated call or visit lifts spirits and chases loneliness away. An act of love and kindness doesn't have to be major to be significant.

Lord, give us courage and wisdom to make a
difference in the lives of those around us.
Also, guide us to notice the blessings
we receive each day.
Amen.

Day 20: The Revived Orchid

He gives strength to the weary and increases the power of the weak.
Even youths grow tired and weary, and young men stumble
and fall; but those who hope in the Lord
will renew their strength.
They will soar on wings like eagles;
they will run and not grow weary,
they will walk and not be faint.
Isaiah 40:29–31

Months ago, I moved one of my nearly dead orchids from the plant stand on the patio to the oak tree behind my house. Friends placed their orchids under a tree when they left for the summer. I decided to try it since the lifeless plant looked beyond help anyway.

I placed it in an old macramé holder and tied it to a large limb. The too-small hanger made the already-dejected specimen hang sideways. At least the dead leaves and crooked roots no longer marred the appearance of my patio. While working in my yard, I would notice the scraggly mess and think of throwing it away. But it remained.

As Hurricane Ian approached, I placed all my potted plants on the patio, lining the wall close to my home. I felt sorry for the excluded orchid, so I attempted to remove the tied hanger from the tree. However, the knot refused to loosen. Since I didn't want to go inside for scissors to cut the thick cords, the plant remained outside to endure the approaching tempest.

Three weeks after the storm, from my window I noticed yellow leaves on the pathetic plant. When I went outside to pluck off dead foliage, three gorgeous, yellow blooms smiled at me. Not only did the orchid survive the gales and torrents of the hurricane for hours and hours, but it flourished. What a beautiful example of God's love and care.

When we face our storms and feel there is no hope, God doesn't give up on us. He can take the broken pieces and create something beautiful that we never imagined.

As people struggle to rebuild and repair the physical damage from hurricanes, God is working to restore their lives with hope, encouragement, and purpose for their discouraged souls.

Abba Father, you are with us even in our distress.
You take the effects of our storms and make them
into something worthwhile.
Thank you for always loving us.
Amen.

Day 21: Waiting for the Storm

Trust in him at all times, O people;
pour out your hearts to him,
for God is our refuge.
Psalm 62:8

After endless broadcasts about the approaching hurricane, all of Florida waited expectantly for landfall. Brightly colored weather maps illustrated possible wind intensity and rainfall. Constantly changing squiggly lines displayed the path of the monster storm. Reports of floods and tornadoes added to the dire predictions.

For days, I occasionally watched weather reports to be prepared but wasn't overly concerned. I secured furniture and plants on my patio. Four chrysalises hung from the top of the butterfly cage, and two caterpillars had plenty of milkweed. Their enclosure sat next to the wall, away from possible rain.

Instead of riding out the storm alone, I decided to leave for my son's home. I thought my house would be safe, but with a few days of heavy rain and raging wind, staying alone would be stressful.

Necessary clothes and other items, like insurance papers and money in a plastic bag, jammed into my suitcase. Food for my family, yarn to crochet small items, an iPad, a cell phone, and chargers went into my car. A stack of books stood at attention on the front seat next to me. I cranked up the air conditioning in the house and locked all the doors. After a glance around the outside of my home, I drove off wondering what I would find when I returned.

Traffic headed in several directions on rain-soaked roads. I merged into the lines of cars to ride out the storm with my family.

As we waited, no one knew how the storm would affect us. Reports of heavy rain, wind, flooding, and tornadoes inundated the airwaves. As Christians, we knew that God was in control. I prepared as much as I could, but the weather conditions didn't change.

Anxiety, adversity, and loss from disasters often bring people together to be kind and helpful. In the middle of our storms, whether physical, emotional or spiritual, we can rely on a faithful God.

Father, be with us in our storms, whether related to
weather or other situations. Thank you for
your love and care.
Amen.

Day 22: Isolated in Another Storm

God is our refuge and strength,
an ever-present help in trouble.
Therefore, we will not fear,
though the earth give way and
the mountains fall into the heart of the sea,
though its waters roar and foam and
the mountains quake with their surging.
Psalm 46:1–3

An eerie silence filled my home when I awoke at 3:00 a.m. Earlier weather forecasts predicted another storm would reach my area between midnight and 2:00 a.m., so I thought I had slept through it. Then a blast of wind slammed into the window by my bed, quickly followed by a deluge of rain pelting all the windows and the roof. Seconds later, a full-fledged tempest assaulted my home. Snuggled under the covers, I intently listened to the rampage.

Finally, I arose and turned on the weather station. A team of forecasters issued warnings, explained maps, and relayed disaster reports. The predicted hurricane surrounded me.

Because I didn't think this storm would be devastating to my inland home in Central Florida, I didn't stay at my son's house as I had done in the past. I now realized my mistake.

I peeked outside as the hurricane raged on in the blackness. My outside floodlights cast beams on a small part of the tempest. Water thrashed through the screen of my lanai. I exhaled as I saw no damage.

After a few minutes of watching the dire news reports, I began my devotional time but couldn't focus. In the middle of the hurricane, a spiritual storm struck me. Loneliness charged into my home. Tears flowed as memories of my late husband, Alan, protecting me surfaced. Grief ambushed me like another hurricane.

In the middle of the night, I connected with a friend on Facebook. We comforted and supported each other from a distance as my tears stopped. Wind and rain continued for hours and hours. After a short nap, I felt less distressed. The feeling of isolation flew away like the wind. Between rain bands, I ventured outside to my porch and checked on two caged butterflies. A quick yet grateful stroll around the house showed no roof damage.

The hurricane had arrived with no one sitting on the couch beside me, but God provided the Bible to comfort me in my distress. Numerous messages and phone calls reminded me of people who loved and cared for me. Just as I weathered the recent hurricane, God has been with me through many other types of storms.

As we face our physical, emotional, or spiritual tempests, we can look to our Abba for comfort and protection.

Loving Father, thank you for providing just what we need as we face uncertainty and loneliness. Be with those who have lost so much in the hurricanes. Help us remember you are our refuge and won't leave us.
Amen.

Day 23: Courage, Not Fear

You will keep in perfect peace those whose minds are steadfast,
because they trust in you. Trust in the Lord forever,
for the Lord, the Lord himself, is the Rock eternal.
Isaiah 26:3–4

Through a break in the trees, a beam of sunlight glowed from shore to shore on the dark lake. In the cool dawn, little clouds swirled over the water. As the sun traveled toward the treetops, an arc of sunbeams joined the dancing mist. The unusual phenomenon captured my attention.

Dewdrops glittered on my flowers. Overhead, wispy white clouds painted an azure sky. After days of drabness, I stared at the gorgeous spectacle. Then the sun exposed another surprise. An expansive spider web hung from the lower limbs of a tall bald cypress standing on the shore. When I walked across the waterlogged lawn, the grass squished with each step. Hours earlier, that area had been part of the lake.

What an incredible sight! For days, constant winds lashed limbs back and forth. Unrelenting rain hammered our state as the gigantic hurricane inched its way to the north. Despite ferocious weather, I gazed in amazement at the spider web that still clung tightly to the towering tree.

The intricate design had several holes, yet the lacework remained intact. Strong anchoring threads held it securely at the top and bottom. Later in the day, I noticed a black-and-orange spider nestled within the woven design.

In the aftermath of the disastrous hurricane, I wondered what we are tethered to. For many people, material possessions were damaged or vanished completely in a moment. Loved ones gone. Homes lost. Cars totaled. Prized belongings destroyed.

Everyone, those who endured the tempest and those who worried about people in the hurricane, suffered in some way. Perhaps worldly goods remained intact, but anxiety, fear, or apprehension took over. Uncertainty about the future brought trepidation.

If God can create spiders who form unyielding webs, he can make strong, courageous people to withstand the storms of life. Life isn't easy, but peace is possible with Jesus.

Loving Father, thank you for being with us in our
storms. Some come from the weather. Others come from difficult
situations around us and from within.
Tether us to you, as you give us peace and strength
for whatever we face.
Amen.

Day 24: Shifting Sands

Be devoted to one another in love. Honor one another above yourselves. Never be lacking in zeal, but keep your spiritual fervor, serving the Lord. Be joyful in hope, patient in affliction, faithful in prayer. Share with the Lord's people who are in need. Practice hospitality.
Romans 12:10–13

All across Florida, people dealt with the devastating effects of Ian. Some minor with only yard debris. However, in nearby areas, flooding continued for months, with closed roads, no clean water, and waterlogged homes. An untold number of people faced the loss of loved ones, homes, and businesses.

The storm churned the waters of the Atlantic and assaulted the East Coast. Sand shifted onto streets, walkways, and lawns. Mounds formed far from the ocean. Prolonged grief and anxiety abounded.

Wind and water altered the shape of the beaches. This storm left a darker, heavier sand, filled with shell fragments that blanketed the usually smooth surface. A stroll on the beach before the hurricane would have left light footprints. However, after Ian, walking became arduous. It took longer to even reach the beach because of numerous closed entrances. Layers of sand covered the walkways.

Each step into the dense sand left deep imprints. With every stride, my heel sank further than usual. The trek along the water reminded me of winter in Indiana after a heavy snow. Each tedious step needed to be deliberate and well-planned. Trails from beachgoers looked like large animals had crisscrossed the shoreline. The mile-long hike felt like ten because of the effort needed to trudge through the leaden mass.

My walk on the beach reminded me that we all face times when superstorms strike and life knocks us around. We struggle to tramp through the mess. But during the battles, we can find hope.

Neighbors and strangers reached out to those in distress. Especially during disasters, we have the opportunity to love like Jesus.

Heavenly Father, come to us in our storms.
Give us the strength to endure
and to help others.
Amen.

Day 25: Troubling Monarchs

*We are confident that God is able to orchestrate
everything to work toward something good and
beautiful when we love Him and accept His
invitation to live according to His plan.*
Romans 8:28 VOICE

Milkweed popped up amid flowers around my house. I welcomed the unexpected plants since I wouldn't have to buy so much for my anticipated multitude of monarchs. After last year's disappointing season with only four butterflies, I looked forward to a repeat of two years ago when over a hundred hatched.

My cousin and I discovered one caterpillar after another on my milkweeds. I gently added them to the butterfly cages. Their voracious appetites kept me busy cutting leaves to feed them. I sighed as I had to clean their cages daily. However, the thought of rescuing them from predators and watching the beautiful creatures flutter around the yard made my efforts worthwhile.

A few days later, two small larvae climbed to the top of the mesh enclosure. Each one began forming its own personal green chrysalis but stopped before finishing. A hint of sadness came over me as both died the next day. Soon after that, four other caterpillars fell to the floor of the cage, curled into balls, and passed away. The situation perplexed me.

When seven chrysalises formed, each one with the gold ring around the center, I rejoiced. I frequently peered into the cage and hoped to see a gorgeous butterfly. Unfortunately, one day a crumpled creature lay on the bottom. Wee legs twitched, but its wings never opened. That happened six more times. Sorrow filled me as I tried unsuccessfully to help them fly.

Although I attempted to protect them, provide plenty of food, and release them into a safe environment, my efforts failed. My yard must have been sprayed with pesticides, which killed them even though I hadn't authorized the treatment. I couldn't control all parts of their life cycles.

Life is like that for us too. We can manage some facets of our lives, but only God has ultimate control. He numbers all of our days. As we depend on him to lead and guide us, we may still face difficult circumstances, but eventually things will work out.

Thankfully, a trio of monarchs did fly around my yard and will hopefully produce more offspring. They remind me that even after an attack and a trial, God gives hope and works things together for our good.

Loving Father, we try hard to control all aspects of our lives.
We know you are the only one who has complete control.
Help us rely on your guidance, love, and mercy.
Amen.

Day 26: The Last Butterfly

The counsel of the Lord stands forever,
the plans of his heart to all generations.
Blessed is the nation whose God is the Lord,
the people whom he has chosen as his heritage!
Psalm 33:11–12

Butterfly cages waited on the patio to be scrubbed and stored for the winter. For months, I diligently searched often for rice-sized butterfly eggs on the underside of milkweed leaves. I enjoyed watching my cages become incubators after I placed the leaves inside and waited for the tiny eggs to hatch. All of the work, though sometimes difficult and demanding, brought pleasure when I watched the process of caterpillars becoming beautiful butterflies.

I waited until the last day of October to prune most of the milkweed plants so the monarch butterflies would migrate to South Florida. However, a couple chrysalises remained at the top of my cage with a few larvae still eating. Each day, I gathered enough food for the late bloomers. They hatched one at a time. When the last chrysalis darkened, the time of its emerging drew near and so did my period of nurturing.

I had mixed feelings as I opened the habitat for the last time of the year. The beauty of the creature fluttering on its own brought a smile. However, I knew I would miss them flying around my garden.

Parents love and care for their children for years, watching them develop and mature. Then one day, the time comes to release their offspring, like my butterflies, into the world. This process of letting go can be faith-testing.

I prayed that I nurtured and taught them well, instilling Christian values and the love of God so they can thrive. Like my butterflies, we must let our children spread their wings and soar into the world.

Loving Father, just as we love our children and try to teach them the right way to live, you do the same for all of us. How comforting it is to know you are with them even when we aren't.
Amen.

Day 27: The Legacy Shirt

The Holy Spirit produces a different kind of fruit:
unconditional love, joy, peace, patience, kindheartedness,
goodness, faithfulness, gentleness, and self-control.
You won't find any law opposed to fruit like this.
Those of us who belong to the Anointed One have
crucified our old lives and put to death the flesh and all the lusts
and desires that plague us.
Now since we have chosen to walk with the Spirit,
let's keep each step in perfect sync with God's Spirit.
This will happen when we set aside our self-interests and
work together to create true community instead of
a culture consumed by provocation, pride, and envy.
Galatians 5:22–26 VOICE

The words on the front of the blue T-shirt proclaimed participation in the Osceola Senior Games. My eleven-year-old granddaughter, Molly, certainly wasn't elderly or even ready to graduate as a high school senior, but she wore one of my dad's shirts as a nightgown. Although she donned his top, she never saw him run track nor play basketball or softball. She only learned of his multiple sports activities from our family stories and pictures.

For years, my dad participated in Senior Games all over the United States, from Florida to Arizona, Pennsylvania to Indiana, and many states in between. Medals, mostly gold and silver, covered a wall of his garage. If he didn't win the gold, he didn't think he had done well. His accumulated supply of T-shirts grew with every tournament. After he passed away, several family members kept a shirt to remember his perseverance in sports and in life.

Even though Molly didn't know him like her sisters did, she carried on his legacy by wearing his shirt. In addition, she has played softball and basketball like he did. Watching her become more like her great-grandpa makes my heart rejoice.

Even though we don't have a T-shirt belonging to Jesus, we become more like him when the Holy Spirit works within us. Instead of a physical garment, we can put on the fruit of the Spirit, which is love, joy, peace, patience, kindness, goodness, faithfulness, gentleness, and self-control.

Our Savior's legacy is even better than a shirt.
Loving Father, guide us as we leave a lasting,
loving legacy for those who follow us.
Help us put on the righteousness of God
as we become more like Jesus.
Amen.

Day 28: Flee Like a Deer

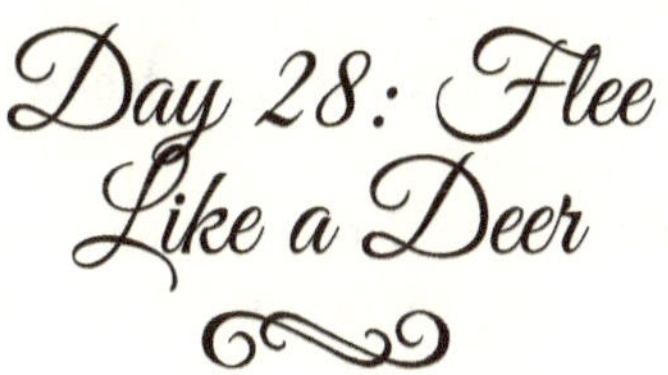

Do not conform to the pattern of this world, but be transformed by the renewing of your mind. Then you will be able to test and approve what God's will is—his good, pleasing and perfect will.
Romans 12:2

As the sun rose behind the forest, I settled into my morning routine on the patio. As I sat with an open Bible and devotionals ready, an unusual movement outside caught my eye. A doe sauntered along my shore in the dim light. Her head turned with megaphone ears pointed toward me.

I became a statue to avoid any sound or motion that would scare her away. She walked a few steps, stopped, faced me again, and turned away to sample fresh needles from one of my cypress trees. At the same time, another deer came into view. I barely breathed as the splendid duo visited my yard for a few minutes. Then, without another glance at me, they continued their morning stroll along the lake.

God made these striking creatures with an especially keen sense of hearing and smell. Their strong legs carry them swiftly from danger. They constantly stop, look, smell, and listen to safeguard themselves from all threats. As soon as they discern possible peril, they flee.

We can learn from the deer. Although our senses of hearing and smell are not as perceptive as theirs, God has given us other ways to recognize possible risks. Do we follow people or ideas that conflict with God's Word? Do we accept the crowd's values instead of standing firmly with God's? Instead of conforming to the world, do we escape from harmful people, activities, and beliefs?

The deer showed how they calmly notice danger and bolt without becoming anxious. What a valuable lesson for us.

Loving Father, show us how to be in your world
but not to be entangled by it. Show us how to
escape danger so we follow your plan.
Amen.

Day 29: The Watery Rut

The LORD had said to Abram, "Go from your country,
your people and your father's household to the land I will show you.
I will make you into a great nation, and I will bless you;
I will make your name great, and you will be a blessing.
I will bless those who bless you, and whoever curses you I will curse;
and all peoples on earth will be blessed through you."
So Abram went, as the LORD had told him; and Lot went with him.
Abram was seventy-five years old when he set out from Harran.
Genesis 12:1–4

Sunlight glistened from the wake of a creature in my lake. The route passed close to the shore, turned, and returned back to the same path. The speed of the critter was too fast for a turtle and the wake too large for a snake. From a distance, I thought perhaps it was a duck, otter or snake bird. Binoculars proved it was none of those.

Day after day, I watched the unusual current but couldn't figure out what caused it. Then my neighbor took a video of the strange movement and determined it was a large carp. The fish's long, shiny body slithered through the water.

Occasionally, a fin sliced the water like a menacing shark. Instead of crossing the lake, it kept circling an area in front of my home.

The creature could have explored the entire lake but remained within a relatively small section. Back and forth it swam but never far from shore. Perhaps food was plentiful there. Maybe other animals stayed away. But the fish never found whether food was more abundant and flavorful near the far shore. What did he miss by staying in the same area?

Perhaps we do the same thing. Instead of venturing into new territories and situations, do we remain stuck with the familiar? Are we afraid to take risks and explore new opportunities?

I don't want to be like that carp caught in a watery rut; instead, I look forward to investigating untried adventures and challenges, whether big or small.

We should not be afraid to venture out of our routine.

Loving Father, show us how to explore and enjoy your world.
There are so many opportunities that we miss
when we are afraid to leave our routine.
Give us the courage to listen and
obey when you lead us.
Amen.

Day 30: A Beautiful Prison

I, the LORD, *have called you in righteousness;*
I will take hold of your hand. I will keep you and
will make you to be a covenant for the people and
a light for the Gentiles, to open eyes that are blind, to free captives
from prison and to release from the dungeon those who sit in darkness.
Isaiah 42:6–7

A young lady led me down a long hallway. Her badge opened the door so I could walk through. "Just let the staff know when you are ready to leave and someone will let you out," she said.

Even though I was locked in, the well-decorated room looked inviting. My friend and another lady sat at a table in a dining area. Her face broke into a huge grin when she spotted me. Her delight warmed my heart.

For over an hour, we talked and reminisced about times when she lived near me. During our conversation, she told me, "I don't want to be here."

I reminded her that she would have to cook, clean, and do dishes if she were at home.

Minutes later, she declared, "I know I need to be here."

Later, she and her friend agreed, "This is a prison. We are locked in."

Even though the facility was clean and looked inviting to outsiders, the residents felt like they lived in a jail. Doors kept them in, but I could walk out.

After I left her section and walked through the assisted living area, four ladies greeted me. They sat on the porch with their walkers nearby while I stood. For several minutes, we visited. Their lives had changed dramatically when they left their homes, gave up driving, and moved into the assisted living facility. They were not locked in, but their circumstances made them prisoners too. On my way home, I thanked God for my home, car, and freedom to go out and do what I wanted to do.

People live in all kinds of prisons. Some are in facilities. Memory care. Hospital rooms. Addictions. Diseases. Wheelchairs. Worry. Fear. Depression. Blindness. Grief. Unforgiveness. Shame. Dementia. Deafness.

Prisons don't always have bars. Circumstances can limit freedom and movement. We might be the cause or perhaps we have no control over our painful situations. Whatever the circumstances, God can use them for his purpose in our lives.

During his time in a Roman prison, the apostle Paul shared the gospel with those around him, and his letters continue to encourage Christians today. God used him in a special way and can do the same for us.

Chains might fall away, in this life or in eternity.

Father, show us how to live in prisons that won't change.
Help us to break out of the ones that we can. Give strength,
encouragement, and wisdom for whatever lies ahead.
Amen.

Day 31: Hidden Sunrise

Cool breezes caressed my face and arms when I stepped onto the patio. After days of sweltering heat, the drop in temperature brought a welcome surprise. Pink-edged clouds emerged from the blackness of night. Behind the forest across the lake, rosy blushes peeked through the trees to announce dawn's arrival.

I looked forward to a glorious sunrise as I read the Bible. A few minutes later, I looked up to see the anticipated spectacle. But it didn't appear as I had imagined.

Clouds formed a gray drape over the sky. Tree limbs swooshed in the wind. Waves swept over the lake in a rush to the far shore. Raindrops pattered on the roof, drenched the grass, and rushed through the long empty downspouts.

A turkey waddled across the lawn to search for safety from the storm. Trees swayed as breezes turned into gales.

Frogs croaked, but no bird melodies rang through the air. My hope for a glorious sunrise never occurred.

Even though I didn't get what I expected, our area desperately needed rain. There was an unforeseen peacefulness in the cool, rainy morning. I pondered the trials I had been facing. I prayed for numerous friends who experienced health and relationship problems. While the rain continued, so did my Bible reading.

We often pray for God to accommodate our requests according to what we believe is best for us. However, he devises an even better plan that unfolds at his discretion. Instead of lamenting that our requests are not fulfilled, we should give thanks, welcome the possibilities, and embrace changes.

Loving Father, even in the grayness of life,
we have opportunities to be thankful.
We can accept the changes with patience
and appreciate what you
have done for us.
Amen.

Day 32: Lessons from the Manatees

I lift up my eyes to the mountains—where does my help come from?
My help comes from the Lord, the Maker of heaven and earth.
He will not let your foot slip—he who watches over you will not
slumber; indeed, he who watches over Israel
will neither slumber nor sleep.
Psalm 121:1–3

A light fog blurred the trees along the bank and formed a filmy curtain that blocked the Florida river's entrance. As the sun warmed the air, the gray mist disappeared, revealing a brilliant blue sky. When river temperatures dip into the sixties or lower, manatees travel from the St. John's River into the warmer waters of Blue Spring each winter.

On my last visit, large gray bodies hovered in the clear water. Occasionally, they drifted upward for a breath of air. Their snouts broke the surface of the water with a puff and then they immediately sank. A few calves remained close to their mothers. Dinky flippers and a large tail propelled the bulky mammals through the crystal-clear spring run.

Crisscross scars from boat motors marred the backs of older ones. Chunks had been taken out of countless tails. Seeing the damage done by humans on these gentle giants saddens me.

Even though seven hundred thirty-six manatees entered the spring that day, none of the docile creatures seemed perturbed by the congestion. No one pushed or shoved. They peacefully floated through the water, ignoring those around them. They also paid no attention to the masses of people chattering and taking pictures from the docks along the river.

As I watched the adaptable animals, I thought of lessons we could learn from them. The massive mammals would never be described as beautiful, athletic, or handsome. They seem to have been created with extra body parts, but they accepted how God made them. Despite their scars, the manatees remained blissful and content. Not one expressed aggressiveness toward the throng milling throughout the spring waters.

Like the manatees, we can find a quiet spot to escape the chaos of our world to enjoy God's creation. In a serene retreat, we can focus on our blessings and ignore distractions. Despite our scars and less-than-perfect bodies, we can learn to affirm the way God made us. When we rely on him, we can use our gifts and skills for good.

Watching the manatees gave me a sense of peace and thankfulness for the numerous blessings God has provided to me.

Creator, thank you for teaching us through your creation.
Open our eyes to all you have done and remind us
that you are always with us and everything you
do has divine purpose.
Amen.

Day 33: Leaving Our Home

Speak out on behalf of those who have no voice, and defend all those who have been passed over. Open your mouth, judge fairly, and stand up for the rights of the afflicted and the poor.
Proverbs 31:8–9 VOICE

For the first eight years of my life, family and friends surrounded me. All of my relatives lived within a few miles and we gathered together often. Then one day, my parents left my brothers, Ken and Joe, and me with some friends for the day. When they picked us up, they shared some unsettling news. My dad got a job as a school principal in a town miles away.

Dad had taught and coached at the first through twelfth grade school that we attended. Being principal at a new school would be a different experience for all of us. I struggled to leave my friends, church, extended family, house, playhouse, and swing set. Everything I had loved, grown up with, and known would be gone.

After searching for a new home, my parents found a rundown house close to the school. They borrowed a few thousand dollars from my dad's brother to purchase it since they had always rented a house.

We lived in the mess during renovations. My grandpa and another uncle used their skills to enclose a porch for my brothers' bedroom. I watched in awe as they tore down a wall in a closet to create a full bath. A third uncle installed a furnace behind a new divider in the dining room. My parents tore off layer after layer of ugly wallpaper from around the house and then added fresh, beautiful paper.

One day, rats visited our back porch. I often wondered if we would ever feel at home in that dilapidated place. Thankfully, with the work completed at the end of the summer, the house began to feel like home and was quite lovely.

Then summer ended. Entering fifth grade at a new school intimidated me. But a girl across the street and her friend graciously showed me around and sat with me at lunch. I noticed other students avoided them and me when I was with them. Perhaps because of one girl's shabby clothes, the duo didn't fit in.

At church, I met new friends and additional neighbors. As time with my newer friends increased, I spent less time with the first ones. Unfortunately, I didn't return their friendship when I made other buddies, even though they had gone out of their way to be kind.

God used that regrettable situation to make me more kind and compassionate toward those who might be overlooked or avoided. He can take our mistakes and ultimately use them for good.

Father, show us how to be more kind. Open our hearts to those around us who need love, friendship, and compassion.
Amen.

Day 34: What Does It Cost?

Do not judge, and you will not be judged.
Do not condemn, and you will not be condemned.
Forgive and you will be forgiven. . . .
Why do you look at the speck of sawdust in your brother's eye and pay
no attention to the plank in your own eye?
How can you say to your brother, "Brother, let me take the speck out of
your eye," when you yourself fail to see the plank in your own eye?
You hypocrite, first take the plank out of your eye, and then you will
see clearly to remove the speck in your brother's eye.
Luke 6:37, 41–42

My first husband's birthday brought memories of our family's breakup many years ago because of his infidelity. That pain from those traumatic events long ago doesn't surface often, but this year the scenario played over and over again in my mind. Even though I thought I had forgiven him and his girlfriend, who later became his wife, pangs of hurt for my children and me returned. A cascade of what-ifs formed in my mind.

Many pastors have preached on the high costs of forgiveness. Some of them are:

- Give up our self-righteousness
- Become humble
- Do not gossip about the offense or offender
- Stop blaming them for what they did
- Stop wondering whether they are happy and hoping they aren't
- Stop reliving the incident over and over again in our minds
- Wish they would ask for forgiveness

As I pondered the exorbitant price of forgiveness, the Holy Spirit brought an image to me. I was lifted from a miry pit and stood at its edge. Muck covered me from head to toe. Without a word, Jesus miraculously wiped away the filth, which revealed a beautiful dress with no trace of dirt. He changed and cleansed me.

Over the years, my life progressed through many stages. There have been times of trials and heartaches, but also periods of happiness and joy. Through it all, God walked with me. How thankful I am for the gifts I have been given.

Unforgiveness holds us hostage.

Forgiveness releases us from bondage and allows us to experience joy.

Only with God can we truly forgive.

Loving Father, thank you for showing me how to
forgive as you walk with me. Guide me to live for
today and not dwell on the hurtful past.
Amen.

Day 35: Blessings Even in Darkness

For what we preach is not ourselves, but Jesus Christ as Lord, and ourselves as your servants for Jesus' sake. For God, who said, "Let light shine out of darkness," made his light shine in our hearts to give us the light of the knowledge of God's glory displayed in the face of Christ. But we have this treasure in jars of clay to show that this all-surpassing power is from God and not from us.
2 Corinthians 4:5–7

Rain slapped the roof of my patio. Wind churned the lake and whipped the trees. Thunder rumbled. What a welcome sound after months of barely a drizzle. I didn't mind a storm as long as rain accompanied it.

The view from my patio last night included brown grass, forlorn flowers, and a shrinking lake. Both the vegetation and I longed for refreshing moisture.

In the predawn darkness, I only heard the crescendo and decrescendo of the rain. Thunder grew louder and closer. But gratitude filled me as the showers increased. Even though blackness blocked my view of the rain, I knew the lawn, trees and flowers devoured the life-giving gift.

Dawn would bring reality to my vision. The lake level would be up. Dust and pollen would be washed away. Leaves would sparkle in the sunshine. Limp blooms would wave. My garden would be cleansed and invigorated.

Even in the darkness, rain restores and exhilarates.

In the same way, we often don't see God working but observe the results. Last week, a friend's recent scan revealed no cancer, even though a previous one showed multiple tumors. A prodigal child calls home and the family is reunited. Peace overtakes anxiety in difficult situations. Kindness appears amid grief. The list could go on and on as we remember.

Just as I am thankful for the revitalizing rain, I am grateful for the blessings God brings, especially during our darkest times.

*Loving Father, thank you for when you work in our
lives in unseen but amazing ways. Help us look for
you and share how you bless us.
Amen.*

Day 36: A Flower and Cookies

*Let no one despise your youth, but be an example to the believers in
word, in conduct, in love, in spirit, in faith, in all purity.*
1 Timothy 4:12 NKJV

A smiling teenage girl stopped at our table in the church café. She held bright yellow and orange flowers in one hand and clutched a large basket in the other. "Would you like a flower?" she asked.

My friend and I each received a lovely blossom from her.

"Would you like a cookie too?" The girl pulled a couple of samples from her basket and told us it was her first attempt at decorating cookies. We each took a bag of slightly imperfect pumpkin-faced treats.

The teen beamed as we accepted her delightful gifts and then left to continue her mission. She circled the foyer to find other ladies to bless.

While I visited with my friend, I ate one sweet and gave the second one to my granddaughter. With no vase, I picked up the sagging bloom before heading to a meeting. During lunch with another friend, the wilting flower waited in a hot car.

After hours without water, my once lovely gift was placed into a container of cool liquid when I got home. Its forlorn head dropped in desperation. Thoughts swirled in my mind. Should I prop it up? Would it be better to throw it away? I decided to leave it alone.

Every time I looked at the pitiful posy, the perky girl who strolled around the church came to mind. She happily dispensed her slightly blemished gifts with a smile.

The following morning, a surprise greeted me. Overnight, the droopy flower gained strength and stood upright in the vase.

Sometimes we feel dejected and downcast, like my bloom. But Jesus can infuse us with his strength and courage.

The flower girl distributed her flawed gifts to equally flawed ladies. We enjoyed the fruits of her labors, and she received the blessing of spreading joy.

Jesus, we thank you for the youth who know you and demonstrate your love to the world. No matter our age, we can learn from those around us, both young and old.
Amen.

Day 37: The Roar of the Leaf Blower

How can a young person remain pure?
Only by living according to Your word.
I have pursued You with my whole heart;
do not let me stray from Your commands.
Deep within me I have hidden Your word so that
I will never sin against You.
You are blessed, O Eternal One;
instruct me in what You require.
Psalm 119:9–12 VOICE

The roar of the leaf blower grew louder as it came closer. A landscaper moved to the rear of my house and pointed the machine at my back step. After a couple of swipes, he walked to my neighbor's house to clear off another clean stoop.

When I looked out front, he had begun waving the blower across tidy sidewalks in front of my home and down the street. The sound of noisy mowers grew as landscapers began cutting the lawns near me. Only then did grass litter walkways.

I wondered why the young man who ran the blower didn't clear the sidewalks after the mowers instead of before them. Later, I noticed that all the grass remnants had been blown away. Perhaps he realized his error and did the job again, or maybe someone else had to take on his responsibility. Either way, the task had to be done twice.

As I shook my head at his puzzling actions, a powerful lesson formed in my mind.

How often do we act before consulting God? We usually think we know what is best and neglect to ask for his instructions. Without his guidance, the results of our actions can be as unsuccessful as the overexuberant landscaper.

If we humble ourselves, listen, and then follow the Holy Spirit's leading, we won't have to repair or redo what we attempted to accomplish on our own.

Heavenly Father, instruct us to ask you for guidance
in our lives, instead of trying to forge ahead with
little counsel and often faulty outcomes.
Amen.

Day 38: An Unidentified Creature

God is our refuge and strength,
an ever-present help in trouble.
Therefore, we will not fear,
though the earth give way and
the mountains fall into the heart of the sea,
though its waters roar and foam and
he mountains quake with their surging.
Psalm 46:1–3

Darkness enclosed my patio like a blackout curtain without even a speck of light. Porch lights beamed so I could read my Bible and devotionals. In the stillness before dawn, I prayed and wrote in my journal.

As summer neared its end, the sun came up later and later. Instead of the shadows of night, I preferred spring and summer when the sun rose earlier and gorgeous sunrises painted brilliant colors across the sky and the lake.

Silence settled all around me. Birds and crickets slept before the sun woke up.

Then, just outside the screen, steps crunched the grass a few feet from me. My heart raced as I froze. A bobcat, bear, or coyote could produce heavy steps like I heard.

Would the animal come through the screen? With the two bright porch lights, the creature could see me clearly. However, even though I stared intently toward the screen, blackness shrouded my vision.

I quietly moved to the sliding door into the house, opened it, and turned on the outside lights. With flood lights gleaming, I scanned my yard but saw no monster. No invader lurked ready to spring at me. No beady eyes stared back. Within seconds, the animal had vanished. No footprints or other clues remained. Only the mysterious sounds lingered in my mind where I envisioned a large black bear roaming around the lake.

As the sun rose, I turned off the lights and continued my devotional time.

Often, our minds imagine scary situations. A tiny problem morphs into a tragedy. What-ifs cause anxiety and can paralyze us as we conceive monstrous scenarios.

Although the mystery had not been solved, I decided to remain on my porch. I could have cowered in fear, retreated inside, and been fearful to venture out.

When we put our lives in the hands of God, we let him take care of the scary stuff.

God, remind us that you are our protector and refuge.
When we become frightened and nervous,
give us peace, comfort, and courage.
Amen.

Day 39: Scary Steps

Humble yourselves, therefore, under God's mighty hand, that he may lift you up in due time. Cast all your anxiety on him because he cares for you. Be alert and of sober mind. Your enemy the devil prowls around like a roaring lion looking for someone to devour. Resist him, standing firm in the faith, because you know that the family of believers throughout the world is undergoing the same kind of sufferings. And the God of all grace, who called you to his eternal glory in Christ, after you have suffered a little while, will himself restore you and make you strong, firm and steadfast.
To him be the power for ever and ever. Amen.
1 Peter 5:6–11

Because of the intense summer heat, I parked far from the store's entrance in a patch of shade. After checking out, I left the store with a shopping cart of purchases and began the long trek to my car. In a flurry of activity, people entered and exited the store and moved about the parking lot to and from their vehicles.

Step by step took me farther away from the bustle of other shoppers to a solitary place in the gigantic parking lot.

Then I heard footsteps behind me. When I sped up, they did too. As I slowed, they slowed. Fear prevented me from looking back and confronting the possible attacker.

No matter what I did, the feet behind me mirrored my cadence. Finally, I stopped completely. Total silence. Surely no one would harm a grandmother in broad daylight.

No one could hear me, or perhaps even see what was happening at such a distance. Were there cameras around? Determined to act normal, I opened my trunk and began putting groceries in my car. Still no sound from my potential assailant.

After loading everything into the trunk, my eyes fell to my feet. Only then did I notice the backless, rarely worn sandals. The flopping of the shoes had mimicked the sounds of someone following me. My mind formed a frightening story that seemed real. Giggling replaced fear. In my laughter, the Lord impressed a lesson upon my heart.

How many times do we create unnecessary worries instead of taking our concerns to Jesus?

Loving Father, when we are frightened and anxious,
make us strong, firm, and steadfast.
Amen.

Day 40: Where Is the Power?

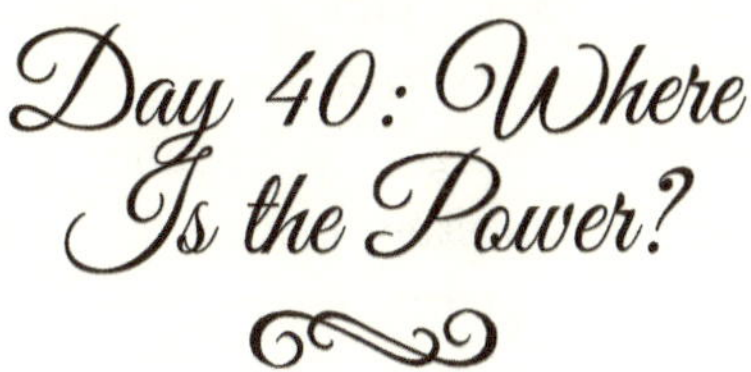

Do you not know? Have you not heard?
The LORD is the everlasting God, the Creator of the ends of the earth.
He will not grow tired or weary, and his understanding no one can
fathom. He gives strength to the weary and
increases the power of the weak.
Isaiah 40:28–29

The numbers on my watch glowed 6:00 a.m. as I climbed out of bed in the darkness. The motion light didn't come on, so I shuffled closer to the door. Still no light. I felt along the wall to the bathroom, where a second motion night light would highlight my way. But it didn't. I flipped the light switch and nothing happened.

No power. Total blackout. Fortunately, I remembered the two flashlights in my closet, which is my safe room, when storms threaten. My hand slid along a shelf and groped for the small light. My finger pushed on the button. Still no light. Back to the closet shelf, my hand found the larger flashlight. Thankfully, the light shone, and the beam guided me through the pitch-black house.

Through a window, I noticed my neighbor's outside light glowing and remembered they had a generator. I opened the front door and stepped outside to see if anyone else had power.

Like a beacon, solar lights illuminated my walkway, reflecting two beady eyes that stared back at me. Upon further inspection, the cage my neighbor placed near my hedge had caught an opossum instead of the armadillo that had been digging in my plants.

At that moment, my outside motion light turned on, which surprised both me and the caged animal. My electricity had returned.

I went inside. A wave of thankfulness washed over me. Light made everything easier. With a steaming cup of tea, I picked up my Bible to read. My hair dryer came on and I watched the local weather report. In the United States, we have become accustomed to constant electricity. Many people around the world do not have that luxury. We expect it and usually aren't grateful.

As the sun rose, I thanked God for the sunlight and the beauty of my lake view. Even when my power was off, his wasn't. He never shuts off during a storm, nor does his energy run out. There is no bill to pay.

Even during my dark morning, I experienced peace and knew that God was with me.

Father, you are with us even when we face dark
and often scary times. Your power gives us
strength and comfort.
Amen.

Day 41: My Birthday Gift from God

My mouth is filled with your praise,
declaring your splendor
all day long.
Psalm 71:8

As morning darkness faded away, a red explosion of color lit up the sky. Vibrant scarlet painted the background of the forest and even the lake. I hurried outside with my phone to capture the magnificent spectacle. However, the camera couldn't fully express the breathtaking phenomenon before me.

From my patio chair, I stared at the transformation of the sky as it moved like the turning of a dial. Crimson became bright orange across the lake while the rest of the sky evolved to pink. In a very short time, pale orange replaced dimness, and then a huge yellow ball peeked through the trees. The pink faded to reveal blue sky with a border of gray clouds. Within a few minutes, I experienced a kaleidoscope of design and color as God presented me with an extraordinary birthday present.

While I marveled at the gift, a curtain of clouds closed to end the production. Although I yearned for a longer display, gratitude flooded my heart for what I received.

Memories filled my mind. Over the years, I have experienced happy periods but also seasons of heartache and grief. In all of them, God has comforted and guided me.

Over the last several years, an increasing number of family members and friends have passed away. With each birthday, I know my time is getting shorter, and I want to make the most of each moment. Age makes me look at life differently than when I was young. Now, people are more important than things. Helping others know Jesus is crucial. Reorganizing my day to spend time with my Savior is a priority. I've learned to overlook insignificant problems, lend a hand to those who need encouragement, and comfort those who are grieving. I'm able to enjoy the beauty of creation around me.

My latest birthday gift from God reminded me of his presence, love, and compassion. The stupendous sunrise was a tiny glimpse of heaven.

Loving Father, thank you for being with us and
giving us special gifts. Encourage and nurture us so
that we notice your presence in creation
and in those around us.
Amen.

Day 42: An Extraordinary Birthday Present

Shout for joy to the LORD, all the earth,
burst into jubilant song with music;
make music to the LORD with the harp,
with the harp and the sound of singing,
with trumpets and the blast of the ram's horn—
shout for joy before the
LORD, the King.
Psalm 98:4–6

A few days after my birthday, I attended a rehearsal for our neighborhood's singing group as we prepared for our Christmas show. After we finished singing, my friend Carol and I walked to our cars and met another couple, Mary and Arnie, who were also looking for their car.

As they looked around for their vehicle, Mary said, "I like your pants."

"Thank you," I said. "I just got them with a birthday gift card from my friend Cherrie."

"Was your birthday recently?" she asked.

"Yes, it was Monday," I answered.

Carol immediately started digging in her purse and told us to wait. She pulled out her harmonica and began playing "Happy Birthday" as the couple sang along. Four senior citizens stood in the middle of the parking lot celebrating my birthday.

Carol told us that she kept a harmonica in her purse so she could play "Happy Birthday" whenever she encountered someone celebrating. She has done it at our clubhouse, in restaurants, and in other places when she notices someone with a birthday.

What fun it was to be part of the extraordinary gift. Getting older doesn't mean you have to be boring or isolated. My neighborhood is full of people enjoying life and making the most of each day, even though we are aging and can't do everything we used to do.

Like Carol, we can all figure out a simple way to share unexpected happiness with friends or even strangers.

Father, thank you for each day and year that you
have given us. Show us how to spread
unexpected joy to those around us.
Amen.

Day 43: Relentless Rain

He stilled the storm to a whisper;
the waves of the sea were hushed.
They were glad when it grew calm,
and he guided them to their desired haven.
Let them give thanks to the LORD
for his unfailing love and
his wonderful deeds for men.
Psalm 107:29–31

Light silently crept to the lake. Raindrops brushed the water and whispered through the trees. For days, clouds and light rain blocked the sun. The previous day brought torrential rain that bombarded the area intermittently throughout most of the day. Evening downpours and winds continued for hours and hours. Moisture sprayed my patio and dampened chair cushions. After weeks of drought, the thirsty grass, trees, and flowers guzzled the precious water.

The dreariness was an adjustment for residents of the Sunshine State who are accustomed to clear azure skies and numerous outdoor activities. For some people, the gloomy weather pushed them into depression. But afternoons inside gave me time to read, connect with friends, and even take a couple of naps. By staying home, there was time to accomplish neglected tasks.

Drab green plants formed clusters outside my porch. But a pot of cheerful, yellow mums inside added a lighthearted touch to the dismal scene.

The days of endless rain reminded me that God is with us in both the rainy and sunny days. During times of despair and heartache, he holds us and offers comfort. In happier seasons, he rejoices with us.

We can look for beams of light and joy, regardless of the difficult situations we face. Jesus gives us hope.

Immanuel, remind us of your love, comfort, and
presence all the time but especially during our
periods of darkness.
Amen.

Day 44: No Shoes and No Feet

He gives strength to the weary and
increases the power of the weak.
Even youths grow tired and weary,
and young men stumble and fall;
*but those who hope in the L*ORD
will renew their strength.
They will soar on wings like eagles;
they will run and not grow weary,
they will walk and not be faint.
Psalm 40:29–31

As I walked across the church foyer to volunteer, I began limping. When I looked behind me, a trail of black fragments followed me. While standing like a flamingo, I pulled off one shoe. A gaping hole replaced the heel.

I hobbled to the information desk and relayed my pathetic story. A lady called the church's man of all trades. Soon, he appeared and assessed my damaged shoe.

"Glue won't help," he said. "But I could tape it."

With one shoe on and one off, I nonchalantly waddled into the volunteers' meeting room with my friend to eat.

Minutes later, my footwear reappeared. Black duct tape encircled the entire back of my sandal. After eating, I stood to join my group, but something didn't feel right. A messy pile of black surrounded my chair. I took my crumbling shoes to the repairman. He smiled.

Another volunteer in a wheelchair offered me her sandals, but they were three sizes too small. While my shoes were missing, I pondered my options. I could hide and refuse to volunteer. Wear too short shoes. Go barefoot, risk embarrassment, and have my toes squashed by hundreds of people entering the doors.

When I thought of our speaker, I knew I shouldn't be self-conscious even if I had nothing on my feet. Nick Vujicic, who was born without arms or legs, inspires millions with his story. He appeals to young and old as he shares the Good News of Jesus all over the world.

How appropriate that my shoes disintegrated just before he spoke. He has adapted to his condition, overcome depression, and now speaks all over the world.

In the past, I would have tried to buy new shoes quickly or perhaps declined to serve. However, being reminded of what's really important has given me a new perspective and helped me ignore the "little things" (including disintegrating shoes) in life.

Heavenly Father, your presence helps us accept difficult situations
and be thankful, especially when we observe
the trials of others.
Amen.

Day 45:
Hearing the Voice

You yourselves have seen what I did to Egypt, and how I carried
you on eagles' wings and brought you to myself.
Now if you obey me fully and keep my covenant,
then out of all nations you will be my
treasured possession.
Exodus 19:4–5

A chorus of birds greeted me when I stepped onto my patio. As the sky transitioned from black to pale blue to pink, I delighted in the beauty and sounds of dawn.

Amid the combination of songs, one overpowered the rest. Frantic screeching broke through the bird symphony. High-pitched squeals joined in the frantic conversation.

With the brightening sky, I identified their resting place. After studying the pine tree intently, I saw two majestic bald eagles flapping their wings within the branches. They lifted themselves up and soared above the forest. One landed briefly on the far shore of the lake. Then both disappeared beyond the trees.

As I pondered the marvelous sight, a sandhill crane bellowed nearby. More melodious songs continued around the lake as dawn turned into day.

If my neighbor hadn't identified the eagle's sound to me one day, I would have missed seeing the birds in the dim light. Without knowing it was an eagle, I would not have studied the tree nor watched for its flight. The magnificent duo would probably have passed by without notice.

What else have I missed while I wasn't listening? When I pray and read the Bible, I try to pay attention to biblical teaching and how I can apply Scripture to my life. Then I am more attuned to what God is doing in my life through creation, his Word, and through other people.

Likewise, when we open our hearts and eyes, we can notice people who need a kind word, a listening ear, or a hug. We can show the love of Jesus.

Dear Lord, help us not be so self-centered that we
miss hearing you. Open our eyes and heart to
opportunities to share your love.
Amen.

Day 46: A Symbol of Hope and Strength

But those who wait upon God get fresh strength.
They spread their wings and soar like eagles,
They run and don't get tired,
they walk and don't lag behind.
Isaiah 40:31 MSG

Though wrapped in a warm blanket, I shivered. Bright sunlight enticed me outside for my morning devotions, where the crisp air rejuvenated me.

The mirrored lake produced a perfect, unblemished image of the surrounding trees. A concert of bird musicians enriched the tranquil scene. Melodies rang out in stereo from around the lake. An amplified solo overtook the other singers for a few minutes. Intermittent tweets and chirps made me smile. Even the bellowing of a retreating sandhill crane added to the chorus.

Ducks floated lazily across the glassy lake. At the top of my bald cypress, a silhouetted hawk waited patiently for a glimpse of his breakfast. A pair of blue herons, with skinny necks extended, swept across the clear sky. A snakebird rose from the water like a cobra, weaving to a flute. Swallows built a nest at the top of a porch column. All were content with their roles.

A white egret followed a dark bird zooming down the lake. When the leader landed in a high pine, I realized it was a bald eagle. He scanned the area, swooped gracefully to the lake, clutched a fish in his powerful talons, and soared away.

Through the years, I had seen eagles across the water but never so near my garden. The strength, beauty, and magnificence of the majestic bird captivated me. What a blessing to see God's creation up close.

I had almost stayed inside but felt a nudge to brave the cool morning. After months of concern and worry about sickness and family members, the spectacular creature refreshed me.

Heavenly Father, thank you for the nudges for us to act.
Encourage us to listen and obey.
Perhaps we will even experience small miracles
like seeing the eagle.
Amen.

Day 47: An Embarrassed Greeter

There is a time for everything and a season for
everything under heaven. . . . a time to weep and a
time to laugh, a time to mourn
and a time to dance.
Ecclesiastes 3:1, 4

The dress went over my head and snuggled too tightly around my middle. Unfortunately, I hadn't tried it on before leaving to spend the night at Chris and Anne's home. "Does it look too tight?" I asked my teenage granddaughter, Ashlyn.

Her sweet disposition wouldn't allow her to say yes. However, her eyes did.

"I brought pants I could wear instead, but I didn't bring a top suitable for church."

"You could look through mine," she said.

I smiled at her generosity. "Thanks, I'm going to wear my dress for church today."

She just nodded with that "whatever you say, Grandma" look.

Surely I would be able to pull my stomach in for a couple of hours. Although I had gained some weight, I didn't think the dress would grip me so tightly. Normally, the draped center camouflaged bulges.

At church, hundreds of people passed me, and many stopped to talk as I greeted them before and after the service. Occasionally, I did remember to *suck it in.*

As I left church with Chris and his family, Ashlyn stepped in behind me. "Grandma, your dress is lower in the back," she said.

My hand went to the neckline in the front of my dress and grasped a tag. *I couldn't have.*

One look at Ashlyn's shaking head confirmed my suspicion.

She stifled a chuckle. "Grandma, you wore your dress backwards."

I covered my eyes and stated with little hope, "Maybe no one noticed."

"Grandma, you were a greeter."

She was right. Even though no one said anything, hundreds of people might have wondered why my dress was on backwards.

I burst into laughter. She cringed and then giggled too.

Advancing age seems to bring more blunders but less concern about how people see me. Instead of being self-conscious, I find humor in many situations. After enduring times of tears, my smiles and snickers returned. If my incident made someone laugh, I'm glad.

Dear Lord, thank you for the various seasons of life.
When we fumble, give us a sense of humor
instead of humiliation.
Amen.

Day 48: Blooms from Brokenness

After you have suffered a little while, the God of all grace,
who has called you to his eternal glory in Christ, will
himself restore, confirm, strengthen, and establish you.
1 Peter 5:10 ESV

Orchids hung from a wooden tower on my patio. Occasionally, I would wheel the stand to different locations, hoping to find more suitable growing conditions. But even with instructions from knowledgeable friends, several of my plants drooped and wilted.

One day, I noticed a long, broken stem that almost split in half. The end of the stalk slumped toward the concrete floor. Even though I planned to prune the dead portion off later that day, I forgot.

For weeks, I noticed the damaged plant during my morning devotions. The injured stem reminded me to grab the clippers to snip it off. But day after day, other tasks demanded my attention, and I forgot as soon as I went inside the house.

While the rest of the plant remained a vibrant green, the end of the partly severed stem turned brown. Surprisingly, after several weeks of total neglect, tiny buds dotted the end of the broken stem and the healthy one near it.

I no longer thought of cutting off the splintered portion but marveled at the revitalization. Buds grew larger on both the fractured stalk and the robust one. Finally, gorgeous purple flowers trailed down both of them.

Watching growth on the fragmented plant became a part of my daily devotional time. God spoke to me through the blooming but injured plant. He reminded me that even in the pain of my shattered life, I could slowly bloom too.

My orchid should not have flowered in its pitiful condition, but somehow it received needed nutrients and blessed me with its unexpected beauty.

According to the world, people in difficult circumstances shouldn't flourish either. However, some of us thrive while enduring painful health diagnoses, grief, divorce, and other heartbreaking trials. Though crushed and shattered, we can find hope, strength, and peace as God revives us. Then we can inspire and comfort others.

Father, thank you for broken plants and shattered
people who bloom because of your love,
compassion, and care.
Amen.

Day 49: God Showed Up

Have I not commanded you?
Be strong and courageous.
Do not be terrified; do not be discouraged,
for the LORD your God will be
with you wherever you go.
Joshua 1:9

The familiar examining room brought tears and too many memories. A couple of years earlier, I waited in the same room with my husband, Alan. But no one sat beside me as I remembered.

When the doctor came in, I pointed out spots on my skin for him to examine.

"No, that one's okay. That one's fine too. If it bothers you, I can remove that one, but it isn't cancer."

My relief quickly turned to concern as he continued, "This one's different. I need to do a biopsy. Call next week for the results." Then he left.

I remembered the malignant sections of skin he removed from Alan's face and body.

Cancer. That hated word brought fear and loneliness. I couldn't share the news with my husband or receive his assurances that I would be fine.

In my car, I hugged the steering wheel and sobbed. Vehicles filled the parking lot, but no one even knocked on the window to see if I was okay.

Combined with the losses of my husband, dad, and mother, the biopsy ignited my fears. Finally, the tears stopped. Reason returned. Numerous family members and friends dealt with skin cancers and all survived.

Before meeting a friend for lunch, I drove by our family's previous home. Just as I turned onto our street, my brother called. I told him about the biopsy and the doctor's visit. He understood my concerns.

He reminded me that a mutual friend's mother still lived near our former house. I turned onto her street and just as I found it, my friend walked out. The timing stunned both of us. Tears started as I explained about my procedure. "God brought us together today," she said as she wrapped her arms around me.

When I felt scared and alone, God supplied people to offer comfort, love, and support. He knew exactly what I needed that day.

Alan's final words continue to lift me up and remind me of God's provision: "Do not be afraid or discouraged. The Lord is with you always. I love you."

God often uses his people to provide just what we need. Sometimes he uses us for others.

*Heavenly Father, thank you for giving us what we
need at the right time. Guide us each day so we can
do the same for other people.
Amen.*

Day 50: The Giraffe and the Clock

And we know that all things work together for good
to those who love God,
to those who are the called
according to His purpose.
Romans 8:28 NKJV

Crash! I watched in horror as the three-foot-tall wooden giraffe plummeted to the tile floor. Its head flew in one direction, and an ear flew in the opposite one.

Instantly, my hands covered my face. Even though I saw the vacuum's electric cord grab the animal's legs as I cleaned the floor, I couldn't stop the fall.

Years earlier, on one of his numerous trips to Africa, Alan had carefully brought the stately figure home in his carry-on bag. I treasured this souvenir as a reminder of his love for African missions.

After the shock wore off, I inspected the broken pieces and picked up the long body.

Thump!

The wooden body hit the dust mop I had been using. It's handle fell against the wall and rammed the wooden wall clock, which my grandfather had made for me years ago.

How could I break two special items from men I loved in a few minutes?

Tick tock.

My anguish turned to shock. For three years, my clock wouldn't tell time or chime. It had become a decoration but not a working clock. But with a smack by the mop handle, the pendulum swung, and a beautiful Westminster chime filled my home.

As I regretted the disfigurement of the giraffe, I marveled at the revival of the clock.

While the clock ticked, I began a repair job on the animal. At Alan's workbench, I found a bottle of glue and hoped it would hold. When the head was stable, I gently reattached the ear.

The restoration of my clock came about because of the brokenness of my giraffe. What I initially thought was a terrible situation had a surprise ending.

Losing my parents, husband, and daughter caused much grief, stress, and pain. However, enduring my losses has enabled me to comfort others who also grieve, which was a surprise.

Dear Lord, thank you for redeeming the pain,
accidents, and stresses we face. Show us how to
recognize those who need comfort and
encouragement.
Amen.

Day 51: A Refugee from the Storm

I will instruct you and teach you in the way you should go;
I will counsel you with my loving eye on you.
Psalm 32:8

Before getting out of bed, I prayed, "Show me someone I can help today."

A hurricane had just ravaged Puerto Rico. Our church had recently held a prayer service for the survivors and took up an offering to provide aid. My heart felt heavy as I drove to the library to volunteer. Few people entered the bookstore as I straightened shelves and added books to the children's section.

Another volunteer, who arrived late, shared about her hour-long wait in bumper-to-bumper traffic. She saw no accidents but several police cars. Then I remembered a news story about locations in Central Florida where hurricane victims could apply for food. One was located near the library, which explained the traffic jam.

As we worked, a dark-haired man entered the store. "Is FEMA here?"

"No, they left last week."

"At the airport, they said we could get help from FEMA. I just arrived last night from Puerto Rico," he continued.

His words broke my heart. My friend and I exchanged looks and moved closer to him.

"Do you know where I can go to find out about housing and a job?" he asked.

My mind tried to grasp his reality. Far away from everything familiar. No job. No home. No family. I couldn't imagine what he had gone through.

I felt God's nudge to reach out to him. "May I give you a hug?"

We embraced briefly. His eyes glistened as he composed himself.

"We are so sorry for what you have gone through," we said.

Neither of us had any real answers, but we directed him to the location where food vouchers were being given out and explained about the long lines.

After he left, we tried to process how difficult life had become for the thousands affected by the hurricanes. Watching videos on the news brought sadness. However, seeing the pain of someone in the flesh fleeing the devastation clutched our hearts.

Even though the hurricanes shattered his island, he wasn't in despair. He requested information but wanted to help himself. I prayed that he got what he needed.

Hopefully, the man felt love and encouragement as my arms gave him God's hug.

Heavenly Father, thank you for the provisions you have given us.
Provide for your children who have experienced tremendous losses.
Enable us to know how we can serve them.
Amen.

Day 52: Another Journey of Grief

You, LORD, keep my lamp burning;
my God turns my darkness into light.
With your help I can advance against a troop;
with my God, I can scale a wall.
As for God, his way is perfect:
The LORD's word is flawless;
he shields all who take refuge in him.
Psalm 18:28–30

Once again, I walked the worn path of grieving with the passing of my daughter, Susie. This time the journey differed from when my parents and husband passed away a few years ago. As I tried to process her death, surprisingly, a sense of peace and relief came over me.

Only then did I understand that my grief for her began years earlier. I longed for her to experience a normal, happy life with her husband and daughters. I mourned over her addictive behavior. The results of her addictions brought disappearances, loss of her family, no holiday gatherings together, not seeing her children flourish, and her family never knowing if she was alive or dead.

After years of prolonged absences marked by only brief visits or phone calls, I learned to protect myself from being drawn into her life of lies and chaos. The long, drawn-out process brought pain, tears, and disappointments. I constantly prayed that God would transform her life.

Over the last few years, she had rarely contacted me unless she was in jail or the hospital. Without drugs, her behavior became more normal. When I saw her in the hospital, she acknowledged she knew Jesus and that she would go to heaven. She wanted the Bible read to her and, with tears running down her face, asked us to pray for her.

When my son and two friends sat with me on Susie's last day in hospice care, my prayer was for her to finally be at peace. She couldn't speak, and her eyes remained closed, but she calmed down and even hummed along to the Christian music that we played near her. Thankfully, that day she peacefully slipped from her chaotic life and met Jesus.

Father, be with those who are caught in the snare of
harmful addictions. Give them the strength to escape.
Hold them and their families in your loving care.
Amen.

Day 53: Alone at the Lodge

Do not be anxious about anything,
but in every situation, by prayer and petition, with thanksgiving,
present your requests to God.
And the peace of God, which transcends all understanding,
will guard your hearts and your minds in Christ Jesus.
Philippians 4:6–7

Mountains rose in the distance as I sat on the deck at the lodge. Rabbits scampered across the lawn. A doe and her fawn emerged from the forest and into the clearing before sprinting away.

Although I was a host for adult guests at SharpTop Cove, a Young Life camp in north Georgia, a last-minute cancellation meant I was alone for two days before other attendees arrived. At first, being by myself in the spacious, wooden lodge disappointed me. But I soon realized the solitude was a gift. My time alone with God allowed me to meditate and explore my feelings of grief.

Sadness came at my daughter Susie's death weeks earlier. But I knew I hadn't fully grieved. Even though my sorrow began years earlier, when her poor choices propelled her into a life of drugs, I mourned for the normal life she never had and how it affected her family.

In her last few months, she read the Bible that I gave her when she was in the local hospital. She tearfully asked for prayers to overcome drug addiction for her daughter and herself. My friends and my son, Chris, talked with her about Jesus, and we all believed she knew Him even though her lifestyle had not changed significantly.

God's peace and joy filled me. Tears sprinkled down my face. I knew then that Susie had been released from a life of pain and turmoil and now experienced contentment with Jesus.

Loving Father, your love and comfort surround us and
take away the pain and disorder of this world.
This is not our permanent home, and
we look forward to being with you
in heaven.
Amen.

Day 54: Not a Gloomy Funeral

Do not let your hearts be troubled.
You believe in God; believe also in me.
My Father's house has many rooms; if that were not so,
would I have told you that I am going there to prepare a place for you?
And if I go and prepare a place for you,
I will come back and take you to be with me
that you also may be where I am.
John 14:1–3 NKJV

Less than two weeks after participating at my daughter's memorial service, I attended and spoke at a friend's memorial.

That morning, funeral and visitation memories crowded my mind. The first one was when I was in fourth grade and saw my first-grade teacher lying still in a box. Flowers, with an overwhelming odor, lined the walls of the funeral home. The whole experience disturbed me.

A couple of years later, during our Thanksgiving dinner with my mom's family, my dad received a call that his dad had passed away. As a sixth grader, I understood a little more about funerals and death, but seeing grandpa in his coffin unnerved me. Tears wove down my dad's cheeks as he stared at his dad's lifeless body. He had always been strong, and I had never seen him cry.

Over the years, more and more relatives and family friends passed away. The tradition at that time was to look at the stiff body, pretend the dead person looked normal, and try to think of comforting words for the family. Often, the casket, open or closed, remained in front of the guests during the ceremony, where it could not be avoided.

People whispered as though the dead might be awakened. Attendees wore black or other dark-colored clothes. Somber music played. A melancholy mood descended on the mourners. The preacher read Scripture and reflected on the deceased person's life. Tears flowed freely amid the grief.

Thankfully, memorial services over the last several years have changed into celebrations. Colorful clothes and joyful music set the mood. Pictures of the deceased and videos of their lives play for visitors. The commemoration of life continues as family members and friends relate stories of the impact the departed had made. Of course, sadness and tears join with smiles and laughter with the focus on life and not death. At the end of Alan's service, we sang "I'll Fly Away." What a joyful ending to his life here and send-off to the next one.

It is hard to let go of loved ones because we miss them deeply. However, if we all know Jesus, we will see them in heaven, which is a reason to celebrate.

Heavenly Father, thank you for being with us in the
sadness of losing loved ones.
We rejoice that those who know
Jesus are with you.
Amen.

Day 55:
Embracing Changes

"Be still, be calm, see, and understand I am the True God.
I am honored among all the nations.
I am honored over all the earth."
You know the Eternal,
the Commander of heavenly armies,
surrounds us and protects us;
the True God of Jacob is our shelter,
close to His heart.
Psalm 46:10–11 VOICE

I stared into the darkness before dawn. Only my patio light allowed me to read my Bible and daily devotionals.

Gradually, trees and bushes emerged along the shoreline. Squawking but unseen birds disturbed my serenity. Patiently, I waited for the morning display.

My anticipation of another breathtaking sunrise grew as the sky came into view. But blue-gray clouds obscured the colorful beauty. Only faint swatches of pink touched the eastern sky, which, like invisible ink, quickly faded.

Though disappointed, I continued to scan the expansive sky. Treasures appeared. Like foam from an ocean wave, a frothy, white cloud traveled over the heavens. Additional crisscrossing lines of white divided hues of gray, blue, and white.

Each time I glanced in a different direction, a new complex picture surfaced to replace the previous one. My eyes went back and forth as I tried to keep up with the evolving designs of the Artist's masterpiece.

My hoped-for sunrise never materialized. However, God provided stunning beauty I never imagined.

Thankfully, I didn't stomp into the house when gray clouds shielded the sun. I would have missed the remarkable beauty and an important lesson.

During my long journey of loss and grief, I have learned to slow down, sit with God, and notice what he provides. I look for him in my despair, rejoice in the surprise blessings, and share what he has done.

Loving Father, thank you for all you do for us.
Enable us to see you and embrace the changes
in our lives even when we anticipated
something else.
Amen.

Day 56: Fleeting Splendors

Eternal One, let me understand my end and how
brief my earthly existence is; help me realize my life
is fleeting. You have determined the length of my
days and my life is nothing compared to You.
Even the longest life is only a breath.
In truth, each of us journeys through life like a shadow.
We busy ourselves accomplishing nothing,
piling up assets we can never keep.
We can't even know who will end up with those things.
Psalm 39:4–6 VOICE

Splashes of pink dotted the dusky dawn sky. The incredible beauty of the heavens touched my grieving heart.

While I concentrated on my writing, the morning sky changed. Pale blue replaced the mauve. The magnificence of the dawn sky remained only in my memory.

The previous evening, I watched the sky dim and darken as a mass of pink tinged the blue-gray billows that swept from west to east. At first glance, the clouds appeared motionless. But while I stared at them, they shifted. Little by little, the wind altered the picture as they continued to move on. Darkness stole the daylight.

In both cases, the splendor of the sky filled my heart and mind. The displays didn't linger but quickly faded away.

While I watched the brief sunrise, I wondered if my recently departed daughter, Susie, watched the glorious splendor from heaven. Was her new home so indescribably magnificent that she wouldn't notice our tiny slice of beauty on earth?

Life is like the fleeting sunrise and sunset. Brilliant for a time and then gone. However, we can strive to make a difference each day. Even lovingly performed simple deeds can change lives, offer comfort, and encourage others.

When we accept Jesus, follow his teachings, and become more like him, we will leave a legacy here and hopefully inspire others to know him.

*Heavenly Creator, the splendor of creation thrills us
and leads us to you. Help us follow Jesus so we can
leave a lasting legacy and then
be with you in heaven.
Amen.*

Day 57: Guidance from Creation

Your love, O Eternal One, towers high into the heavens.
Even the skies are lower than Your faithfulness.
Your justice is like the majestic mountains.
Your judgments are as deep as the oceans,
and yet in Your greatness,
You, O Eternal, offer life for every person and animal.
Your strong love, O True God, is precious.
All people run for shelter under the shadow of Your wings.
Psalm 36:5–7 VOICE

My focus waned. As the sky transitioned from black to pale blue, I stared at the changing design. Stripes of white crisscrossed the eastern sky. In the south, strips of dark clouds variegated the azure canopy. Near the horizon across the lake, yellowish beams peeped between the trees.

The ever-changing view mesmerized me and distracted me from reading the Bible and finishing my devotionals. Then I realized that experiencing and appreciating the front-row seat to God's creation would be my worship that day. To sit quietly, be grateful, and enjoy the presence of God was the most important thing I could do.

Ducks quacked and swam around the serene lake. Tiny birds fluttered from tree to tree in the dimness of dawn. Spanish moss swayed from bare cypress trees. A trio of large sandhill cranes flew high above the forest. Cardinals chirped a greeting. A ball of light blazed through the woods onto the dark water.

While immersed in God's creation around me, I escaped the pressures, pain, and perplexity of our unsettled world. Our Creator provides food for the ducks, birds, and fish. Plants receive needed nutrition, moisture, and sunlight. Not only is he faithful in providing for plants and animals, but for us too.

Even amid all this beauty, I noticed a few dead plants by the lake and in my flower beds. Tiny shoots grew at their feet. A legacy to the ones passing away brought hope.

Just as cycles occur in the plant and animal worlds, we also face seasons of life. Some are joyous and delightful. At other times we face disappointment, discouragement, and despair. Even during those periods, God remains faithful to stand by us, grasping us tightly when we can only hold on by a tiny strand, and promises never to leave us.

Often my instructions come from reading the Bible, but that day, God guided me by observing his magnificent creation. Thankfulness flooded me with a sense of wonder.

We can find a spot outside or near a window to sit silently and observe as we learn to be more grateful.

Creator God, I can't thank you enough for all you
have given us. Even in the hardest times, we can
depend on your peace, presence, and comfort.
Amen.

Day 58: The Disappearing Egret

Test me, Lord, and try me, examine my heart and my mind;
for I have always been mindful of your unfailing love
and have lived in reliance on your faithfulness.
Psalm 26:2–3

From my kitchen, I glanced toward the lake. In the cool but sunny morning, the long neck of a great white egret rose above the shoreline while the bank concealed his body.

His elongated neck stretched out, and bit by bit, his torso caught up. The majestic creature stood like a statue, his eyes scanning the dark water for a tasty breakfast. Cautiously, the slender neck lowered behind a mound of plants at the lake's edge.

The giant egret's presence and movements begged to be written down, so I spent a few minutes writing about him in my journal. When I looked up, he remained hidden behind the partially dead foliage.

My eyes looked right and left. No sign of the stately bird. Time passed. I stood up and stared toward the lake in all directions. I expected him to pop up from his hiding place. He didn't.

By then, I realized the egret had disappeared while I was writing. His abrupt departure disappointed me since I always enjoy watching wildlife from my patio. However, my shifted attention prevented a satisfactory end to an engaging story.

Instead of writing during the experience, I could have waited to pen my devotional, even though some details might have been lost.

How many times do we become distracted and miss the important things?

Think of what is most significant in your life. Are you giving that top priority?

*Heavenly Father, you constantly provide beauty
around us, but we don't always notice because we
are too busy. Teach us to examine our lives and see
whether we prioritize what is truly important.
Amen.*

Day 59: An Abundance of Weeds

*I have told you these things, so that in me you may
have peace. In this world you will have trouble.
But take heart! I have overcome the world.*
John 16:33

Warmer weather drew me to my weed-infested yard. Why do weeds continue to flourish when desirable plants do not? Bags filled as I pruned off dead branches, picked up fallen twigs, and yanked stubborn invaders from three sides of my home.

A few days later, I decided to tackle the remaining section. With a burst of energy, I pulled on a pair of gloves and pushed my wheelbarrow filled with garbage bags, shovels, and a bucket to the far side of my home. A green carpet covered the mulch all along the house.

I plopped down on the ground and began tugging at the unwelcome greenery, placing them into my large container. Over and over, I got up to dump the pail's contents into a black garbage bag.

Sweat dripped as I moved inch by inch toward the end. Spiky pineapple blades scratched my arms when I yanked on weeds growing near them. When I stared at the remaining invaders, I wanted to throw my gloves down in defeat. My back ached, my parched throat longed for water, and dirt clung to my clothes.

However, when I glanced at the portion I had finished, a sense of accomplishment filled me. Compared to what I had already done, only a small section remained.

Life brings challenges and obstacles that seem crushing. Sometimes, quitting appears to be the only answer. But when we remember what we have overcome, the future can be less daunting. Encouragement overtakes despair.

When I pray for peace, strength, and wisdom, God leads the way. A Bible verse comes to mind. A call or visit brings hope. A sermon teaches. A song calms.

On earth, we will face troubles, but we have an eternal Helper to get us through.

Lord, give us peace and strength to face struggles.
Help us remember how you have gotten us through
tough times in the past and promise
never to leave us.
Amen.

Day 60: Grief at the Grocery

Groceries filled one bag after another as the customer placed her parcels into the cart. No one spoke as she and the clerk bagged her items. She was out of breath as she moved to pay.

"Are you okay?" I asked the obviously stressed woman.

"No. My friend just died. Her family came, and there is no food for them. I just wanted to do something."

My heart broke. Every time I hear of someone losing a loved one, my heart hurts.

When we left the store, I told my granddaughter, Molly, "I have to give her one of my books."

I looked across the parking lot, but the lady had disappeared. I scanned the area and was ready to give up when she appeared from behind her car. Before we reached her, she headed back into the store. Molly and I hurried to catch her, but again she eluded us.

We branched out to search the store, and I saw her on a nearby aisle. I moved as quickly as I could without running through the store. Finally, I reached her. "I just saw you in line. I am sorry about your friend. I wrote a book on grief and wanted you to have it."

Tears came. Two strangers hugged as Molly watched.

"Isn't it amazing how God works?" I said to my special granddaughter as we left the store.

She gave me a high five as we both felt the joy of helping a grieving lady. We praised God for how he used circumstances for us to see and minister to her.

The grieving lady needed kindness in her pain, and the Holy Spirit led us to be like Jesus.

Loving Father, thank you for arranging our encounter
by nudging us to help a stranger.
Help us listen and, with our actions,
be more like Jesus.
Amen.

Day 61: From Barren to Beautiful

Be joyful in hope, patient in affliction,
faithful in prayer.
Share with the Lord's people who are in need.
Practice hospitality.
Bless those who persecute you;
bless and do not curse.
Rejoice with those who rejoice;
mourn with those who mourn.
Romans 12:12–15

After his diagnosis of idiopathic pulmonary fibrosis, Alan announced that we should sell our large dream house, downsize, and move to a place where life would be easier for me. Even though we struggled with the news of his impending death, we both realized it was the right decision.

Alan and I tramped through sand to decide on the right spot for our new home. Only a few lots remained along a peaceful lake. Seven spindly cypress trees stood on the shore, but a forest enclosed the opposite side. Even with the barrenness of the homesite, we saw our future dream and decided on the lot.

A little over eleven years later, the view changed dramatically. The tall cypress limbs reached out to hug each other. A tiny oak grew into a towering shade tree and home for a variety of wildlife. Green grass formed a carpet over the sandy soil. Multicolored flora edged the shore and bordered the house. Building a new home helped distract us from the reality of Alan's terminal disease.

During that time, both of my parents went into a rehab facility and then to my brother and sister-in-law's home to receive twenty-four-hour care. My dad passed away before we moved, and my mother's health declined.

Alan and I looked forward to getting involved in our new neighborhood together. But that didn't happen. His health quickly deteriorated, and four months later, he passed away. My family and friends offered love and comfort. My life changed drastically.

As I navigated widowhood, my once desolate home site became a much-needed sanctuary of peace and comfort. God took barrenness and created something beautiful.

My life didn't turn out the way I hoped. However, God used the pain, burdens, and troubles to create something new. Despite tribulations, I have been loved and blessed.

Loving Father, even in our hardest times,
you provide for us and bless us in amazing ways.
Thank you for never leaving us,
even when we feel hopeless.
Amen.

Day 62: Extending the Legacy

Even when I am old and gray,
do not forsake me, my God,
till I declare your power to the next generation,
your mighty acts to all who are to come.
Psalm 71:18

Volunteers, seated at high tables, ate fruit, potatoes, bacon, and biscuits. We waited to begin connecting with members and visitors coming to the early church service.

One of the youngish pastors stood before the group and explained our duties. Before he prayed, he looked at me and asked, "Do you want me to embarrass you?"

Before I could answer, he said, "This is Rebecca Carpenter, Chris Storms's mom, who will be serving with us."

Smiles. Murmurs of welcome. Acknowledgment of my son surrounded me. Most of the volunteers in the room were young enough to have been my children. For them, I was probably just a random senior citizen until they learned about my son.

Only one pastor and his wife in the room knew me from years earlier when I started attending the church. At that time, I was active in various activities and knew many people. Chris was only known as my son.

Over time, difficult situations, a longer drive to church, and less energy caused me not to be as involved. I giggled to myself as Pastor Jeff introduced me as Chris's mom. Because Chris, Anne, and their daughters were active members of our church and involved in many activities, they became well known by many people. The role reversal was part of God's plan. As the older generation steps back, the younger ones take over.

How thankful and blessed I am to see the gradual transition of roles. I am not yet ready to quit, but have engaged in several new opportunities and ministries myself. I have watched Chris and his family grow in their involvement. What an encouragement to see my grown son, his wife, and their family now being recognized for their acts of service in the church.

Heavenly Father, thank you for children who continue
the family legacy to their own children
as they share about you.
Amen.

Day 63: The End of the Story

Don't fret or worry.
Instead of worrying, pray.
Let petitions and praises shape your worries into prayers,
letting God know your concerns.
Before you know it, a sense of God's wholeness,
everything coming together for good,
will come and settle you down.
It's wonderful what happens when Christ
displaces worry at the center of your life.
Philippians 4:6–7 MSG

When my granddaughters were young, Ashlyn, Emily, and I would settle down on the couch in their living room to watch one of their favorite movies. I snuggled in, prepared to be entertained. Soothing music accompanied the dramatic opening scenes in Clearwater, Florida. Memories of my time on that very same beach there during my college days surfaced.

Curled next to me, Emily provided commentary for the show. "This part is funny," she said over and over.

"Emily, don't tell Grandma what's going to happen," her older sister Ashlyn admonished.

Talking ceased. Three sets of eyes stared at the television. The riveting tale completely engrossed all of us.

"Oh, no!" I exclaimed when something bad or troubling happened. Emily would turn and smile at me.

Unexpected trials. Difficult situations. Heartbreak. One after the other. Some scenarios hit too close to home. Their problems were similar to my friends' problems. Surprisingly, neither of the girls seemed affected by the troubles like I was.

At one point, tears trickled down my face. Emily gazed into my watery eyes but did not comment. Instead, she said, "Grandma, you don't know the end of the story."

Later, resolutions came to the characters as they overcame obstacles. Smiles and laughter returned both on the screen and in the living room.

My anguish and tears didn't change the outcome, but they did decrease my enjoyment. Ashlyn and Emily knew that things would work out in the end, so they didn't despair.

Like the movie, life is crammed with unforeseen and unsettling circumstances. Desperation, loneliness, and failure appear to determine the ending. It is easy to get depressed with unpleasant situations, but Emily's words apply not only to the movie but also to life.

As Christians, we know the director and producer who resolves conflicts and makes all things new. When faith and trust replace fear and worry, the tough spots are easier because God knows the ending even when we don't.

Heavenly Father, guide us as we struggle through life. Strengthen our faith and trust in the one who knows our life story.
Amen.

Day 64: Welcoming the Lonely

For it is by grace you have been saved,
through faith—and this is not from yourselves,
it is the gift of God—not by works,
so that no one can boast.
For we are God's handiwork,
created in Christ Jesus to do good works,
which God prepared in advance for us to do.
Ephesians 2:10

The list for the monthly potluck dinner in my neighborhood included only one other single.

Do I want to go with so many married people?

I hesitated, but then added my name.

Several unfamiliar faces greeted me when I entered the room for dinner. Thankfully, I noticed some residents I knew and walked to their table. Unfortunately, all seats at their table were taken.

People claimed chairs at most of the tables. However, at the far end of the long room, one couple sat alone. With my bottled water in hand, I maneuvered toward them. "May I join you?" I asked.

They smiled and said, "Yes."

As we exchanged names, a lady sat down beside me. Another couple asked to join us. We learned that all of them were newcomers except for me. We talked for a while and I discovered the woman sitting beside me was a recent widow who had come alone too.

On the way to the clubhouse that evening, a radio pastor said to look for the lonely and hurting. His words directed me to join a couple sitting by themselves, which allowed me to make new friends.

Because of my journey of grief, I understood loneliness. With gratitude, I stepped out of my comfort zone to welcome and encourage my tablemates.

God directed my steps and thankfully, I followed His plan.

Heavenly Father, help me to listen and obey
when you guide me to do something
that isn't easy.
Amen.

Day 65: Seeing Clearly

Therefore if you have any encouragement from being united with Christ, if any comfort from his love, if any common sharing in the Spirit, if any tenderness and compassion, then make my joy complete by being like-minded, having the same love, being one in spirit and of one mind. Do nothing out of selfish ambition or vain conceit. Rather, in humility value others above yourselves, not looking to your own interests but each of you to the interests of the others. In your relationships with one another, have the same mindset as Christ Jesus: Who, being in very nature God, did not consider equality with God something to be used to his own advantage; rather, he made himself nothing by taking the very nature of a servant, being made in human likeness.
Philippians 2:1–7

White dotted mounds of green glittered in the bright sunshine. Gleaming insects flittered above the lake. White spots on slender stems waved in the breeze near the water. Tall trees topped with masses of emerald quivered in the wind.

"

Nothing in my view of the lake was clear. After cataract surgery, my eye's clarity for distance declined. Only glasses brought faraway objects into focus.

Since I remembered my crystal-clear sight after LASIK several years ago, I assumed the outcome of cataract surgery would be the same. Unfortunately, that did not happen. Eye drops and glasses helped but did not solve the problem. Of course, I longed to see better but learned to adapt.

As I looked out toward my lovely view, I knew I did not see its actual beauty but only a blurry image.

What else have I missed? Do I observe the pain and hurt in eyes around me? Do I discern who could use a hug or a word of encouragement? Do I neglect to share with people who are searching for Jesus? Do I pass by someone when I should stop to check on them? None of these situations would improve with eyeglasses.

Perhaps busyness, selfishness, or lack of confidence clouds our field of vision and distracts us from what God wants us to do. When we pray for God's direction, the eyes of our hearts can see more clearly with love and compassion.

Father, help us to truly see and care for those we come in contact with, including those we know well and those we meet briefly. Guide us to follow your will.
Amen.

Day 66: The Man with the Sign

Keep on loving one another as brothers and sisters. Do not forget to show hospitality to strangers, for by so doing some people have shown hospitality to angels without knowing it. Continue to remember those in prison as if you were together with them in prison, and those who are mistreated as if you yourselves were suffering.
Hebrews 13:1–3

The light turned red. A man holding a wrinkled, folded-up cardboard sign stood between lanes of cars and looked sadly into an open car window. When he shuffled to the median next to me, I remembered there was a bag for such a situation in my car.

I reached behind my seat to find it in the nest of cloth shopping bags. Miraculously, I grabbed it on the first attempt. I held the bag out to the man in weathered clothes as he neared me while the light remained red.

"Thank you," he said as he looked at the bottle of water and the granola bar in the bag. "That man . . . He said horrible things . . . I have to go lie down." He couldn't finish.

My heart broke as tears glazed his eyes.

"I am not a bad person. I don't steal."

We locked eyes. The light changed and we moved apart forever.

Why did the driver of the car ahead of me feel he should berate the guy who hadn't yelled or been disrespectful or violent? But he voiced upsetting words to an already forlorn fellow. The consequences of his actions would never be known to him, but they devastated his target.

All the way home, the sadness and tears of the anguished soul burdened my heart. No matter what caused him to stand on the streets hoping for handouts, he was still a man loved by God. He didn't deserve the verbal abuse.

The homeless aren't always treated badly, but more often ignored. Overlooked as though they are nothing. No matter the circumstances people find themselves in, we can be kind and show the love of Jesus.

That man and I will probably never see each other again, but I hope our brief interaction gave him a bit of encouragement and hope.

At home, I started filling plastic bags to give out when needed. Of course, a smile and a kind word are readily available without a bag.

Loving God, show us who needs a kind word,
a smile, and encouragement.
Guide us to help those who are
in difficult circumstances.
Amen.

Day 67: Night of Laughter and Dancing

This is the day that the Lord has made; let us rejoice and be glad in it.
Psalm 118:24 ESV

Close to six hundred teen campers, leaders, staff, their families, and adult guests formed a long procession down a dirt road to a western-themed night. Everyone dressed for the occasion at SharpTop Cove, a Young Life camp, in Georgia.

The teens had no idea what awaited them at the end of the road. But when they arrived, the fun began. Carnival games had been set up for them to play and win tickets. They shot basketballs into baskets, footballs through hula hoops, set up bottles with a loop on a stick, knocked blocks over with a ball. After they won five tickets, they could throw a pie into their leader's face. Five more tickets and they could spray the pie off with a water hose.

Aromas of popcorn and cotton candy wafted through the crowd. The outing brought laughter as country music played. After students experienced the carnival, they were instructed to form two lines: one of boys and one of girls. They circled behind a small barn and came out the front. Couples were formed randomly from the two lines of teenagers and instructed to sit in groups of sixteen. The announcer told them to ask their partner where they were from and get to know each other while they waited for everyone to pair off.

Four couples demonstrated how to do a simple square dance. Campers stood and began the Virginia Reel. When a dancer became confused, others helped out. They laughed and moved down the line. Students came from Texas, Tennessee, Indiana, Ohio, Louisiana, North Carolina, and Spain. They came from affluent neighborhoods and the inner city. Black and White. The differences didn't matter. They grabbed hands and danced.

Probably most of them had never square danced. But they joined in and had fun with people they had never met.

When I watched the group, my heart filled with love. Unlike the world we had escaped for a while, no one was left out. No one put anyone down for being different. Hundreds of young people enjoyed being kids.

With no phones for a week, the teenagers focused on being present. I prayed that they would remember the joy of camp and how to love each other and God.

*Loving Father, continue to be with those who
attended camp and help them see how much
you love them. Change lives and strengthen
the faith of those who accepted Jesus.*
Amen.

Day 68: Self-Sacrificing Friends

Some men came carrying a paralyzed man on a mat
and tried to take him into the house to lay him before Jesus.
When they could not find a way to do this because of the crowd,
they went up on the roof and lowered him on his mat
through the tiles into the middle of the crowd,
right in front of Jesus.
When Jesus saw their faith, he said,
"Friend, your sins are forgiven."
Luke 5:18–20

My week at the Young Life camp in Georgia immersed me in the lives of teens. Watching the young people learn about Jesus and help each other touched my heart. Their welcoming warmth, which they showered down upon me as a grandparent figure, encouraged me.

During our week, a group of special needs teenagers joined the able-bodied ones in the activities. One young lady sang the national anthem a cappella for over six hundred people before dinner one night. The crowd cheered when she finished.

When a young man in a wheelchair entered the clubroom with his friends, they helped him get down the steps to join the other students. At the end of the program, they retrieved his wheelchair and whisked him away. Those same friends made sure he enjoyed all aspects of camp. During western night, he was placed in line for the Virginia Reel. Partners swirled around him so he could participate in the dance.

The following day his friends accomplished something I didn't even try. A long, steep climb to the top of the mountain gave trekkers an opportunity to see an incredible view. The hike was known to be challenging, but the young men endured the journey while carrying their friend in a sling over two poles on their shoulders. They ignored their own obstacles to give him a view from the top.

Their selfless actions reminded me of the men who lowered their friend through the roof to be healed by Jesus. But instead of lowering him that day, the teen boys carried their friend upward to experience Jesus.

I will remember the young men who sacrificially assisted their friend all week to make his camp experience as meaningful as theirs. They truly displayed the love of Jesus and served with no desire for recognition.

Loving Father, show us daily how we can serve
sacrificially. Bless the young people who care for
others and provide a beautiful
example to follow.
Amen.

Day 69: Answer to Prayer

And whatever you do, in word or deed,
do everything in the name of the Lord Jesus
giving thanks to God
the Father through him.
Colossians 3:17 ESV

Whenever I travel, I always pack a couple of my books and I pray to meet people who need words of comfort.

On my flight home from Indiana, a gray-haired lady sat by the window as I took the aisle seat. We spoke briefly. Then, as more passengers filled the plane, another older lady moved into the middle seat.

I learned the woman next to me had visited family for three weeks and was ready to return home to The Villages, a huge retirement community an hour from me. She'd lived in Indiana with her pastor husband before moving to Florida.

Once in the air, both of us turned on our tablets and became immersed in our games. She touched her screen and looked at me. Free Cell came up on both tablets. While I continued trying to win, she jumped from one game to another.

Later, as we sipped our drinks and ate teeny airline snacks, we talked more. She relayed her husband had died three years ago and the previous day was their anniversary. I understood how difficult special days could be. Our conversation continued with stories about our deceased husbands.

I handed her my book on grief. She looked at it and tried to give it back.

"No, it is for you. I wrote it," I said.

"You wrote it?"

Most people don't believe they are talking to the author. I assured her that I had written it and told her how God comforted me during my darkest days, and I always pray for someone who needs a copy.

At baggage claim, she invited me to visit her home so she could show me around. I have no idea if we will meet again, but I am confident God placed her in my life that day.

God is faithful. Over and over, I have met and shared hope with grieving people on planes, at church, in parking lots, and throughout my day.

Loving Father, thank you for answering prayers.
Help us notice people around us who need a listening
ear, a kind word, or even a book to ease their pain.
Amen.

Day 70: Lake Mary Champions

Start children off on the way they should go,
and even when they are old
they will not turn from it.
Proverbs 22:6

Yellow-shirted fans cheered loudly from the stands. Back home in Florida, watch parties celebrated each game. Cheers erupted as the player slid into home plate for the extra-inning run to win the final game.

During the series, the Little League boys from Lake Mary, Florida, played hard and didn't give up even when they were behind. The entire community and beyond Central Florida rejoiced at our state's first-ever World Championship win.

After losing to Texas, the double-elimination tournament provided a second chance. They beat Texas in a later game but consoled the losing team before celebrating.

During every game, the team displayed their love for baseball, their families, and each other. When they traveled to Pennsylvania to play baseball, they didn't forget to be kind and compassionate to their teammates and opposing teams.

Immediately after scoring the winning run in the final game, they demonstrated how to be true champions. When the boys saw the tears of the losing Chinese Taipei team, the Florida team put their arms around the players and offered comfort. Their coach squatted down to console a devastated Chinese player. Their kindness brought tears to my eyes as I watched boy after boy support their rivals before jumping and cheering their win.

They were global Little League titleholders but, more importantly, champions in the way they lived. Interviews with parents during the series showed families who loved and cared for others.

As adults, we can learn how to live well by emulating the actions of the Lake Mary Little League champions both on and off the field.

Loving Father, help us remember to be kind and loving
to those around us, even if they are different from us.
Turn enemies into friends.
We can often learn from children.
Amen.

Day 71: The Monster Storm

In my distress I called to the Lord;
I cried to my God for help.
From his temple he heard my voice;
my cry came before him,
into his ears.
Psalm 18:6

Menacing clouds concealed the approaching dawn as Tropical Storm Helene approached the Caribbean, rushing toward Florida. Schools closed. Activities canceled. Most Floridians remained at home to wait for the storm.

Continuous weather reports replaced normal programming. Colorful maps displayed possible paths and the intensity of the storm. But no one could accurately forecast when, where, or how strong it would be. We learned the mammoth hurricane would cover most of our state, in addition to several northern ones.

All day I waited and watched. Sprinkles fell on the lake and strong breezes ruffled the trees. After my phone blared a tornado warning, I hurried to my safe room, a large interior closet. The weather map showed a twister only a few miles from my home. When evening approached, instead of expiring, our day-long tornado watch extended until the following morning. Wind whipped the trees. Lights flickered.

Surprisingly, even with the gales and torrents, I slept through the night and woke after the watch expired. I listened for evidence of the disturbance but heard only silence. The sun shone brightly outside.

Newscasts showed horrible scenes of devastation in Florida, Georgia, North Carolina, and beyond. While I slept, the hurricane raged and altered lives. Helene's fury continued to the Midwest and Northeast. Flood waters rose and caused unimaginable destruction.

The power and strength of the gigantic Category 4 hurricane exceeded all others. No one predicted its path accurately. Thankfully, people came together to help. First responders saved desperate folks. Power company workers restored electricity as soon as it was safe. Shelters opened. Ordinary people helped neighbors. A newscaster, doing a live broadcast, stopped and waded through water to rescue a woman trapped in a flooded car.

As weeks, months, and years of repairs continue, may we not forget and assist those who have lost so much. We should also show the same kindness, compassion, and love to those around us because no one escapes the storms and trials of this life.

Heavenly Father, only you know when the storms
will come and where they will go. Show us how to
deal with them and how we can help others.
Amen.

Day 72: An Unpredictable Week

Have mercy on me, my God,
have mercy on me, for in you I take refuge.
I will take refuge in the shadow of your wings
until the disaster has passed.
Psalm 57:1

What a difference a week makes! A fiery ball illuminated the sky. A forest of green enclosed the mirrored lake. Breezes tickled leaves and purple flowers. An occasional bird melody drifted through the air. Peace and tranquility hovered over my retreat as sunlight glistened on the pond.

The previous week with Hurricane Milton presented a much different picture. Winds battered trees for hours. Clouds replaced the sun. Not one squirrel, bird, or deer ventured out. No melodious songs broke the spell. Continuous storm-filled news reports caused anxiety.

Uncertainty abounded as our state prepared for the worst. Residents and tourists watched and waited. I had endured other hurricanes, but Milton caused a new level of fear and apprehension all across Florida and beyond. The winds increased rapidly, as we watched the monstrosity expand and head toward us.

Even with Hurricane Milton advancing, my daily time with God brought me peace. Residents had endured the devastation of Hurricane Helene a week earlier. Hundreds died as a result. Thousands lost their homes and businesses, but they persevered with an outpouring of assistance and compassion from people around the world.

The beauty and serenity of my lake reminded me that God protected us in the last storm. I prayed and felt a sense of calmness, unlike the hyped newscasts. I knew God promised to be with us and never leave us.

Heavenly Father, we weep with those frightened and
overwhelmed by the hurricanes of life.
Surround them with peace and compassion.
Thank you for all the workers and first responders
who have labored to support and encourage
thousands of people in multiple states.
Thank you for being with us in our storms,
whether physical, mental, or emotional.
Amen.

Day 73: Frenzied Dragonflies

Peace I leave with you;
my peace I give you.
I do not give to you as the world gives.
Do not let your hearts
be troubled and
do not be afraid.
John 14:17

Sunlight shimmered on the mirrored lake. Dragonflies darted in a frenzy near the shore, up to the trees and back out across the water. Individually and in small groups, they rose, dipped and circled but never stopped to rest.

Birds seemed more relaxed. A pair of cardinals perched in my oak tree and chirped a cheerful welcome to the dawn. An unseen duo played a game of rhythmic follow the leader. The first one near my house would utter a specific tone and rhythm. From across the lake, the same tones and rhythms were repeated. For several minutes, they continued their back-and-forth joyful chants.

After I finished my morning devotional time, the lake's peacefulness held me captive. Instead of rushing inside to start my daily tasks, I delighted in the beauty before me. I thanked God for my home, the lake, safety from the hurricanes, and the wonder of perfectly created flowers and trees.

Too often, I am like the frantic dragonflies who dash from place to place and miss the charm and wonder around me. It is easy to ignore the blessings when I focus on problems.

My yard isn't perfect but I can overlook brown leaves, algae on the lake, and bare spots in the grass to appreciate the splendor of my retreat.

Eventually, I must leave the tranquil sanctuary and return to the reality of normal life with its complications. However, I try to recognize God in the messiness of life just as I do in the grandeur.

God of Peace, show us how to slow down,
reflect, and appreciate all you have given us.
Your peace comes even in difficult situations.
Amen.

Day 74:
Restroom Meeting

The one who blesses others is
abundantly blessed;
those who help others
are helped.
Proverbs 11:25 MSG

"I can match your pace," the lady in the wheelchair told us as we walked beside her at the retreat center. My steps quickened, and she sped up until we reached the meeting room. My friend and I laughed as we tried to keep up with her.

The next day, she wheeled up to us, but her smile was missing. "Do you know where there is a restroom?" she asked.

Patiently we guided her. After maneuvering through difficult doors and a narrow doorway, the wobbly seat in the handicapped stall made her afraid of falling and she wasn't able to use it.

While we found the second restroom, my friend left to find a maintenance worker. "I know another one," I said.

We hurried to another building and down a hallway—but then my hand grasped a locked door. She kept saying that it was okay. I knew it wasn't by looking at her face.

"Let's try one more building," I said.

We managed to get her into the last restroom through a set of swinging doors. There was no way she could have gotten through on her own.

"Thank you so much," she said.

"Even though you said, 'It was okay,' it wasn't."

She nodded.

On our way back to the meeting room, we talked briefly about her life. Polio had put her into a wheelchair as a child. During that same time, I received the new vaccine to prevent the dreaded disease.

"My husband died four years ago," she said.

"Mine died three years ago," I replied.

Later, I handed her one of my books on grief and briefly explained my story.

"I want to give you a hug," she said. "God brought us together."

I agreed as I bent down to embrace her. Two widows. Almost the same age. One with polio and one without. Why was she affected and I wasn't? Her positive attitude, in spite of her difficulties, inspired me. God knew our encounter would be a blessing for both of us.

Heavenly Father, thank you for all the encounters
you arrange for us. You bring people together to
bless each other, and sometimes
strangers become friends.
Amen.

Day 75: Blessing in the Bookstore

Each man should give
what he has decided in his heart to give,
not reluctantly
or under compulsion,
for God loves a cheerful giver.
2 Corinthians 9:7

How old are you?" the lady asked my granddaughter Emily, who had her head buried in a book.

Surprised at the interruption, Emily looked up from her reading. "Eleven."

"Do you babysit? I used to enjoy it when I was your age."

"No, not yet," Emily said.

The stranger held up a children's financial book. Emily nodded in appreciation. The lady left the store.

Emily returned to her favorite pastime—reading. As a youngster, each Sunday after the church service, she retreated to the bookstore until her family summoned her to go home.

Minutes later, the lady approached Emily again. "God told me to give this to you," she said as she held out her hand with money in it.

Emily noticed bills in the stranger's hand. "No, you don't have to do that."

"Please let me bless you," the lady said as she placed eleven dollars on the open book Emily held.

My granddaughter was ready to refuse again, but she told me later that her mom's words came to mind: "If someone wants to give you something, graciously accept it." "Okay. Thank you," Emily replied.

She quickly found her parents and relayed the amazing story. With a few dollars added from her dad, she purchased a girl's devotional book that her mom had planned to buy for her.

We all marveled at what the unknown customer did for a child she didn't know.

Because the lady felt the Holy Spirit's nudge and acted on it, the blessing for Emily rippled to a host of other lives. How many others, inspired by her kindness, will continue to spread the blessing? She certainly inspired me.

Loving Father, thank you for kind strangers.
Help me heed your Spirit and
be a blessing to others
that I meet.
Amen.

Day 76: The Highway Racket

A tender answer turns away rage,
but a prickly reply spikes anger.
The words of the wise extend knowledge,
but foolish people utter nonsense.
The Eternal can see all things;
His gaze is fixed on both the evil and the good.
Proverbs 15:1–3 VOICE

In the predawn darkness, I settled into my wicker chair on the porch. For an hour or more, my mind focused on the Bible as I read with my lamp illuminating it.

When the sun rose, my attention turned to the calm lake, lofty trees, and gorgeous flowers. White African irises opened overnight and formed a floral display under the cypress trees. Bees buzzed around the orange tropical sage and dipped into the bell-shaped blooms. A hummingbird plunged its teeny beak into the orange flowers too.

Then irritating highway noise broke my concentration. The racket grew louder as drivers rushed to unknown destinations. Rumblings and revved-up motors competed with high-pitched motorcycle engines.

The traffic clatter drowned out soothing bird songs. Squirrels hid in safe trees. Butterflies ceased flying. Flowers lost their luster when my mind focused on the noise. The wonder of swimming mallards dimmed. The harsh, unwelcome uproar swept away the tranquility of my lake retreat.

The understanding that highway commotion negatively affected my outlook made me think about the daily disturbances that can influence our lives. If we listen to constant bickering and words that divide, we join the din. Reading negative reports and arguing captures thoughts and leads to unreasonable actions.

I realized we should limit contact with toxic people who bring us down, like we should limit unhealthy food, activities, and pollutants. I can't stop traffic noise on the interstate or from other people, but I can control how long I focus on it. When I pay attention to the serenity of my sanctuary, I hardly notice the noise.

If we focus on God and his teachings, we have more peace, greater contentment, and less anxiety. The Bible is an instruction book on living a life more like Jesus's.

Loving Father, guide and instruct us in the way we should live.
Help us focus on you and your teachings
instead of the chaos of the world.
Amen.

Day 77: My Tranquil Cocoon

His house is my shelter and secret retreat.
It is there I find peace
in the midst of storm and turmoil.
Safety sits with me in the hiding place of God.
He will set me on a rock, high above the fray.
Psalm 27:5 VOICE

Frothy waves tumbled to the shore from the expansive ocean. A fiery ball rose from the water and created a brilliant path of light from the cloudy sky to the beach—pockets of blue burst through the haze.

From my sixth-floor balcony, I looked down on a miniature world. Birds, hidden within palms and palmettos in the beachside park, sang sweet-sounding songs. A few walkers meandered along the boardwalk amid the foliage. Gopher tortoises peeked out from their homes. Early risers strolled the shore. Sunlight reflected from the car windows off and on like the lighthouse across the inlet. Surfers ventured into calm water to attempt to catch a wave but their rides were short.

The peaceful scene enthralled me and encased me like a tranquil cocoon. If only I could remain in my serene refuge to escape the tragedies of the world.

From my vantage point, I didn't encounter reality. No arguments or unkind words drifted to my ears. Distance blinded my eyes to glares and frowns. Everything below me looked charming and blissful.

Even though the idyllic panorama remained the same, my focus changed. Not seeing nor hearing the tensions and problems did not erase them. Hurtful conversations and angry words remained. However, my ears also missed kindness and loving words. No hugs or kisses could be observed from the height of the balcony.

The people below me drifted away as I rested and relaxed in the beauty of God's creation. Soothing ocean waves and an azure sky brought assurance. There will always be trials and chaos in our world, but amid them, God provides peace, comfort, and healing.

Father, thank you for the beauty that surrounds us
even when we experience challenges.
Give us shelter with encouragement,
peace and hope even during
our tribulations.
Amen.

Day 78: Unwelcome Clouds

Clouds formed a veil across the sky above the ocean. White capped waves rushed to the shore. Dreariness shrouded the entire beach and nearby park. Only a few walkers ventured onto the shoreline or boardwalk through the nature preserve. Three lonely cars were parked on the almost deserted beach.

At dawn, a sliver of gold glittered through a break in the clouds. The brightness lingered briefly and disappeared when the curtain closed the gap. Haze crept closer and closer to the shore.

A day earlier, a gorgeous sunrise welcomed the morning. Light illuminated the beach and ocean. Rows of cars lined up along the packed beachfront but away from the waves. Surfers ventured into the water to find the perfect wave.

The huge contrast between days reminded me of life. Happiness fills one day. Suddenly, everything changes because of a terrible event. Fear and anxiety overcome joy.

Sometimes we face the undesirable consequences of our own actions. However, difficult situations may also hit us without warning and demolish our peace and normalcy. In every circumstance, we need to remember that God is with us in the challenges. He offers comfort, guidance, and encouragement during the pleasant days and the incredibly burdensome ones too.

Sunshine can be fleeting but so are the clouds. Neither will last forever but all are part of life.

Loving Father,
help us maneuver through each day,
whether easy or hard,
in the strength and peace
you give us.
Amen.

Day 79: Festive Flower

Let us not become weary in doing good,
for at the proper time we will reap a harvest
if we do not give up.
Therefore, as we have opportunity,
let us do good to all people,
especially to those who belong
to the family of believers.
Galatians 6:9–10

A server at a restaurant I frequented didn't smile like normal when she came to my table.

"Are you okay?" I asked.

"This is the anniversary of when my husband passed away," she said.

I told her that I understood. We then shared our stories of grief.

"I will pray for you," I said when I gave her a signed copy of my book on grief.

That Christmas, my granddaughter Molly and I took her some homemade cookies. Every time I visited the restaurant,

I looked for her. And while making up vases with flowers to give to friends, I knew she needed one.

"These are for you," I said when I handed her daisies before my friend, Sallie, and I sat at a nearby table.

She smiled. "Yellow is my favorite color. Thank you so much."

While Sallie and I ate, the grateful lady kept thanking me and checking to see if there was anything we needed.

As we ate our custard, she returned. "The flowers are beautiful," she said. With her hand over her heart, she continued, "But you noticed me. You thought of me. I wasn't just a lady cleaning tables."

Her words touched my heart. I just wanted to make her smile with the flowers, but the gesture went much deeper.

I often talk to people who serve me in the community—stores, restaurants, doctors' offices. However, when I am in a hurry or distracted, I'm sure I make them feel invisible.

Her heartfelt words convicted me that small acts of kindness can make a huge difference. To love and serve like Jesus, we need to be aware of those around us. A kind word, a smile, or a vase of flowers might change someone's day.

I am thankful I listened to the Holy Spirit's nudge that day.

Holy Spirit, help us notice those who may be feeling
lonely and unappreciated. Instruct us and open our
hearts to love others.
Amen.

Day 80: An Unconnected Loner

So do not fear, for I am with you;
do not be dismayed, for I am your God.
I will strengthen you and help you;
I will uphold you with my righteous right hand.
Isaiah 41:10

On my daily walk, I noticed a single sandhill crane by the sidewalk. The stately four-foot gray birds often frequent my neighborhood, but that one was unusual. Instead of walking the streets with a mate and two youngsters, it roamed alone.

Each spring, pairs of cranes stroll our neighborhood with two offspring since both parents care for their young. After hatching, the colts resemble fluffy ducklings but soon their legs lengthen and they look more like the adults in color and size.

Parents teach them to root for food in the grass. The foursomes wander from yard to yard. Most residents enjoy their visits except when they stand in the middle of the street and hold up traffic. Laws require motorists to stop for our feathered friends.

Because of identical coloring, I couldn't tell whether the solitary crane was male or female. Every time the bird appeared, I scanned the area for other companions. Unfortunately, none appeared. The offspring would have matured and taken off. Since sandhill cranes mate for life, its partner must have died. The lonely fowl walked alone.

The bird searched for food but appeared downcast. No calling to its mate with loud squawkings. No flapping of wings or looking around, just trying to survive, ambling, and moving one clawed foot in front of the other.

I can understand the devastation of losing a loving spouse. A partner is gone. Missing. A part of the heart is ripped out.

But thankfully, we aren't alone if we believe in Jesus. He holds us tightly and gives peace. Strength comes when we feel we have none.

God often sends people into our lives to offer comfort and friendship. Some become special friends and others may become new partners who ease the loneliness.

The troubled crane reminded me of how grateful I am for Jesus's constant provision and companionship. Dealing with my heartbreak and sadness has increased my faith and helped me comfort others facing their own heartaches.

Father, you give us what we need during our periods
of loneliness, grief, and pain. But you don't leave us
alone in our challenges.
Amen.

Day 81: Genuine Love

Most of all friends, always rejoice in the Lord.
I never tire of saying rejoice.
Rejoice!
Keep your gentle nature so that all people will know
what it looks like to walk in His footsteps.
Philippians 4:4 VOICE

Lifts lowered wheelchairs to the ground. Special friends departed in buses and vans. Camp staff lined the sidewalk and cheered arriving campers. Every special needs young person arrived with a buddy for three days.

Young people from all over Florida came to Young Life's Capernaum Camp, nestled in the Ocala National Forest. Some traveled for hours to attend the weekend retreat. Adult leaders, along with college and high school students, gave up a long weekend to unconditionally love and serve their friends.

During the first evening's carnival, music played. Dancers crowded the area. Games and popcorn added to the festivities. Plates of whipped cream were thrown onto the leaders' faces. Excitement filled the air.

My eight-year-old granddaughter, Molly, and her friend worked at the temporary tattoo table. Every person selected a design. The young girls held wet paper towels over each decal until it was set. Meanwhile, the line of students lengthened.

As more people came, I started helping out. One young man picked out a tattoo from the designs I showed him. While I held the paper towel on his arm, he looked at me tenderly. Without a word, he placed his hand over mine until the color was secure. Tears pricked my eyes.

Though I was there to help him, his touch of kindness soothed my heart. He never spoke but continued to smile. Then he was gone and off for more fun.

That evening began three days of love and service. I marveled at the dedication of the buddies and how they tirelessly helped those who are often rejected or ignored by society. The joy and smiles of each friend and buddy touched my heart over and over.

Loving Father, thank you for showing us how to love
and serve people who are different from us.
How precious to experience the beauty of serving
and loving unconditionally.
Amen.

Day 82: Sky-Blue Comfort

*Praise be to the God and Father of our Lord Jesus Christ,
the Father of compassion and the God of all comfort,
who comforts us in all our troubles, so that we can
comfort those in any trouble with the comfort
we ourselves receive from God.*
2 Corinthians 1:3–4

Before Alan died, he composed a lengthy list of things to do before he passed away. It was not a bucket list but tasks to accomplish to make my life easier when I was alone.

For example, he wanted me to have a new car. At that point, his health had deteriorated and he required oxygen. He called dealerships near us and explained that he was dying and wanted to buy a car for his wife without playing games.

The first salesman didn't seem to care. The next one introduced himself and kindly assisted us. He showed us several cars. Then I spotted a sky-blue Camry. It drove well and seemed like the perfect car for me.

Alan never drove the new car because his strength had declined. A month later, he passed away.

Even after twelve years, I think of him every time I drive my car. The trustworthy vehicle has over 135,000 miles. I am not ready for a new one, and I'm not sure when I'll ever be.

I remember the many times my blue car surrounded me as tears of grief fell. It protected me when a vehicle rammed me on the interstate. In parking lots, my sky-blue sedan stands out in a sea of white, gray, silver, and black, making it easy to find.

From a distance, my car looks new, but up close, scars, dents, and scrapes are evident. The windshield has been replaced twice because of flying rocks on the highway.

But as my car ages, so do I. We have both encountered damage, endured hardships, and faced storms. Scars and dents remain, but we continue running.

When life seems too hard, we can see how God has been with us in our storms and continues to be with us no matter our age.

Father, you are always with us in all kinds of circumstances.
Guide and comfort us as we go through our trials
so we can comfort others.
Amen.

Day 83: Over a Month Late

Oh, the depth of the riches of the wisdom
and knowledge of God!
How unsearchable his judgments and
his paths beyond tracing out!
"Who has known the mind of the Lord?
Or who has been his counselor?"
Romans 11:33–34

Colorful blooms in my garden announced the arrival of spring. Yellow coreopsis, white periwinkles, and orange salvia replaced foliage browned by the cold of winter. Tiny pineapples sprouted from circles of dark green leaves. Clumps of dainty African irises expanded near the house and by the lake. The growth around my yard delighted me.

However, my Easter lilies hadn't made their usual appearance. In fact, one plant had been flattened by a landscaper's heavy boot. The forlorn stem remained on the ground with no hope of revival. Another lily, planted near my oak tree, sprouted upward with healthy green stems but no buds. In past years, my festive lilies bloomed near Easter. Never had they not blossomed. I thought of buying a new one but never got around to it.

As I prepared for our Resurrection Day meal, I forgot about my non-blooming lilies. The holy day lunch with my family and friends took precedence over my plants. We enjoyed the day with much laughter, delicious food, and an entertaining egg hunt. No one missed my broken and non-producing lilies.

Weeks passed. One day, I glanced toward the tree and noticed my lily growing taller and taller. Buds appeared at the top. I watched daily to see the late bloomer's progress. A single blossom unfurled. The following day, the second one burst open. Not long after that, the final two displayed their beauty.

Four large, white trumpet-shaped flowers crowned the top of one slender stem. They proclaimed their presence with a lovely elegance. Because I had become accustomed to the familiar flowers around my yard, the appearance of the lilies enthralled me. Day after day, I marveled at their growth. Even though they were not present for Easter, God brought them to me at just the right time so that I would not be distracted by the other flowers.

We often plead with God to work out our plan on our schedule. When that doesn't happen, we may become discouraged or disheartened. However, his answers and timing are the best for us.

Lord, guide us and give us patience as we wait
for you to answer our petitions.
You know what we need
at just the right time.
Amen.

Day 84: We Need a Bible Story

Even when I am old and gray, do not forsake me, O God,
till I declare your power to the next generation,
your might to all who are to come.
Psalm 71:18

"Grandma, let's play a game," said seven-year-old Ashlyn with pleading eyes.

"You have to brush your teeth first," I answered. "It's almost time for you to go to bed."

After a song and prayer, our toddler, Molly, snuggled down with her baby doll. Then I concentrated on the two older girls, Emily and Ashlyn. I knew the game had to be short to get them to bed on time.

"As soon as the game's over, you have to go to bed," I reminded them. I knew their nightly routine of reading a book, singing, reading the Bible, and praying. However, I hoped we could skip a few steps.

Our *Uno* game began. Five-year-old Emily and I gathered a fistful of cards while Ashlyn's decreased. I realized the game would not end before their 8:30 p.m. bedtime. Attempting to set an end time, I interjected, "After one more round, we have to stop. Whoever has the fewest cards wins."

Reluctantly, they agreed. Ashlyn won.

I hurried them off to bed, prayed, and kissed each girl. "Goodnight. It's past your bedtime."

With the door closed, I sighed. But as I walked away, a little voice summoned me.

I opened the door. "You aren't supposed to call me after you go to bed."

"But, Grandma, we didn't read a Bible story," Ashlyn said sadly.

"We played a game and now it is time for bed," I reminded them.

Emily added, "I won't go to sleep until Mommy comes home and reads a Bible story."

Knowing my granddaughter's stubbornness, I relented. She definitely would not go to sleep, which would be worse than being a few minutes late.

"Grandma, the little Bible has stories that are only two pages," Ashlyn offered.

Quickly, I found the verses about Noah. The girls could have recited the story by heart. After I read the accompanying prayer, they were satisfied.

Two more kisses and the light went out for a pair of happy girls, and a grandma who received a sermon from her granddaughters.

If only we as adults were so adamant and faithful in reading our Bibles each day.

Father, teach us to love you and the Bible.
Thank you for using young children to teach us
and remind us of the importance of being
in your Word every day.
Amen.

Day 85: Filling a Need

> "I was hungry, and you gave me food to eat.
> I was thirsty, and you gave me drink.
> I was a stranger, and you took me in.
> I was naked, and you clothed me.
> I was sick, and you visited me.
> I was in prison, and you came to me."
> Then the righteous will answer him, saying, "Lord, when did we see
> you hungry, and feed you; or thirsty, and give you a drink?
> When did we see you as a stranger, and take you in;
> or naked, and clothe you? When did we see you sick,
> or in prison, and come to you?"
> The King will answer them, "Most certainly I tell you,
> because you did it to one of the least of these
> my brothers, you did it to me."
> Matthew 25:35–40 WEB

As I rummaged through plastic containers looking for crochet hooks, a lady with a broken leg stared at me. In the crowded thrift store, we stood alone in the craft area.

Finally, she spoke. "I'm a teacher and getting things for my class."

"I was a teacher for almost thirty-seven years," I said.

Together, we found buttons and needles for her students at a small Christian school. Her eyes wanted to tell me her story, but her lips only said, "I never thought I would be doing it for so little. I've already spent more than I should have."

She hugged me before she left. I picked up buttons and other craft supplies.

At the counter, my new friend looked through her overflowing cart while I paid for my purchases. "This is for you." I handed her several black buttons and some money.

Her face lit up. She thanked me and we hugged. I hoped to make life a little easier for a struggling teacher. Her enthusiasm warmed my heart.

While we talked, another customer pushed a cart full of toys to the register. She spoke to the clerk. "Every time I come in here, I look at a certain Bible. I hope the price goes down more so I can get it."

She left, and minutes later it hit me. I should have bought her the Bible. For me, the cost was nominal but to her a luxury. The missed opportunity nagged at me.

Even though I cheered up the teacher, my visit to the thrift store convicted me because I missed blessing the second lady. Over the years, how many opportunities slipped by?

Father, guide us to be more loving, compassionate,
and helpful. When we sense a need,
whether large or small,
help us fill it.
Amen.

Day 86: Surprise Grandeur

*I will give thanks to you, L*ORD*,*
with all my heart;
I will tell of all your wonderful deeds.
I will be glad and rejoice in you;
I will sing the praises
of your name,
O Most High.
Psalm 9:1–2

As the day lightened, the ebony sky gave way to dusty blue in tiny bursts of color. Shadowy trees developed into colorful woods around the lake.

With the dawn, birds awoke and joined together in a musical choir. Their singing became louder and louder as the sun rose and glittered on the lake. Frogs added their deep percussion rhythms to the singers.

A bit of pink glowed behind a lofty pine tree. Instantly, an explosion of coral infused the eastern sky. Rosy splashes splattered southern clouds. No words could describe the breathtaking expanse of the heavens.

I simply sat and stared in awe. The morning gift fascinated me. The loveliness and surprise grandeur provided a sense of reverence, harmony, and serenity.

Too soon, the deep pink expanse faded to pale rose and finally to off-white. But with the color changes, a collection of clouds swept over the sapphire sky. Fluffy. Small. Large. Filmy. Endless. A vast stretch of heavenly beauty with no discernible movement captured my attention as I studied the transformation of the heavens.

The tranquility and wonder of the dawn exhibition reminded me of God's work in my life. He often surprises me with more than I ever expected. He brings positive changes that I might not notice except when I look back. I need to reflect on what he has done for me in the past and take time to enjoy what is given to me each day.

Creator, thank you for the amazing displays of your creation
that we see each day.
Remind us of the many blessings we receive and
help us appreciate what you do for us.
Amen.

Day 87: Listening for the Voice

DEMONSTRATE Your ways, O Eternal One.
Teach me to understand so I can follow.
EASE me down the path of Your truth. FEED me Your word
because You are the True God who has saved me.
I wait all day long, hoping,
trusting in You.
Psalm 25:4–5 VOICE

A mass of swirling clouds danced across the dark lake. The wisps rose and twirled as dawn awakened. Cypress trees stood like soldiers protecting the forest. Not a leaf stirred on trees or flowers. Except for whirling fog above the water, all movement ceased. Normal life halted.

As the sun rose, fog deepened and further disguised the lake and trees. Bit by bit, the scene before me disappeared before my eyes. I looked toward the gray expanse and finally saw slivers of tiny ripples.

A solitary, boisterous crow broke the silence with his annoying caws. Then he flew away. Quiet returned.

From across the lake, squealing chatter erupted. I searched without success to see the majestic birds. Their shrill shrieks continued for a few minutes before finally ending. Haze prevented me from observing the bald eagles. During the summer, they perch in trees across the lake. Neighbors along the shore text whenever someone observes them.

A friend taught me to recognize the voices of the birds. With careful observation, a listening ear, and much patience, I often enjoy their presence.

Hearing God's voice also takes observation, a listening ear, and perseverance. He speaks through his Word as I read my Bible each day. I notice him as I study his creation. Sometimes, he instructs me through a sermon, a book, or another Christian. The more I know him, the easier it is to identify his voice.

Another way he speaks to me is through my writing. I see a situation and instantly notice a lesson that I write about. Often, I am the one who needs the teaching. When I was younger, few messages came to me. Was it because I wasn't paying attention or because he wasn't showing me anything? I am not sure, but probably because I wasn't attuned to him.

Teacher, show us how to listen intently
when you speak. Open our eyes, ears, and hearts
each day in all situations so that
we can follow your plan.
Amen.

Day 88: Productive Seeds

And so finally the sower scattered his seeds in a patch of good earth.
At home in the good earth, the seeds grew and grew.
Eventually the seeds bore fruit,
and the fruit grew ripe and was harvested.
The harvest was immense—
30, 60, 100 times what was sown.
He who has ears to hear, let him hear.
Matthew 13:8–9 VOICE

Swaying flowers nodded in the gentle breeze. The ones I planted formed a lovely garden around the bird feeder. White and purple periwinkles flourished and spread out. Portulaca wove a pink and white carpet in front of the periwinkles.

However, the garden extended to more than I had carefully planted. On the other side of the lawn, three-foot-tall sunflowers loomed above all other plants. They smiled at the lake with their bright, yellow faces. Fan-shaped palmettos gathered at the base of a pine tree. Tiny white blooms vibrated as the wind rustled their leaves.

I am not sure how most of the flowers appeared around my garden. Probably birds dropped seeds or the wind dispersed them. Sunflowers sprouted from birdseed scattered from the birdfeeder. I had not planted my surprise flowers but they matured, formed seeds, and spread out to nourish birds and hopefully produce more flowers.

Isn't that what we do? By living Christian lives, we produce seeds that are strewn into our world. A few are gobbled up to provide nourishment and encouragement. Others may be washed away or blown with the wind to eventually sprout or die. Thankfully, a number of them find the perfect environment to grow, prosper, and multiply.

Kernels we distribute can be a hug, a kind word, or a listening ear. Often, people silently watch our actions and form opinions. Therefore, we must carefully sow good seeds instead of weeds. What productive seeds can we sow today?

Creator, show us how to sow fertile seeds and
not give up when there is no harvest.
Over time, planting one seed after another may
finally reap an abundant crop.
You are the one who causes growth.
Amen.

Day 89: Flourishing at Senior Fest

The righteous will flourish like a palm tree,
they will grow like a cedar of Lebanon;
planted in the house of the Lord,
they will flourish in the courts of our God.
They will still bear fruit in old age,
they will stay fresh and green,
proclaiming, "The Lord is upright;
he is my Rock, and
there is no wickedness in him."
Psalm 92:12–15

Cars and buses dropped off adults at Lake Yale Conference Center. Attendees ranged in age from their mid-fifties to the mid-nineties.

For years, I attended the retreat with friends for a time of peaceful relaxation. The conference center overlooked a large lake away from the bustle of life. Flowing Spanish moss draped towering oak trees in the style of Old Florida. Hammocks waited under shade trees for participants to rest. Over three hundred Christians from Florida and surrounding states gathered as we escaped the chaos of the world at the serene camp.

During the conference, talented musicians blessed us with traditional hymns. The songs flooded my mind with childhood memories of services in small Indiana churches. A variety of speakers conveyed messages that touched hearts and souls. Comedians entertained us with their antics. Gospel singers delighted the audience with joyful renditions.

Staff members and volunteers from around the United States served attendees with constant smiles. Golf carts provided rides for those who had trouble walking. Men transported luggage upstairs. Servers carried trays of food for people who needed assistance.

An assortment of classes covered a wide selection of topics. Then came more activities such as a movie, art class, golf games, relaxing along the lake, or walking throughout the camp. Some campers took a restful nap. During the retreat, all the workers lavished the love of Jesus onto participants and each other which refreshed us to return to our normal lives.

As senior adults, we could sit at home and do nothing productive. However, if we are still here, God has something for us to do. We can sing, laugh, and not take ourselves too seriously.

The conference strengthened my faith and inspired me to serve others better.

Lord, we may not be able to do what we used to do.
As we age, help us flourish and use our skills, gifts,
and wisdom to serve others well and
expand your kingdom.
Amen.

Day 90: Deeply Rooted Oaks

To comfort all who mourn, and
provide for those who grieve in Zion—
to bestow on them a crown of beauty instead of ashes,
the oil of joy instead of mourning,
and a garment of praise instead of a spirit of despair.
They will be called oaks of righteousness,
a planting of the LORD
for the display of his splendor.
Isaiah 61:3

At the garden's entrance, a group of senior adults from my church waited for other members to arrive. O.A.K.S. meant Older Aged Kingdom Saints. However, we preferred to be called "Oaks," deeply rooted and full of wisdom.

Free admission brought lines of cars to Leu Gardens, an oasis nestled in busy Orlando. Older folks joined moms with babies and tots in strollers. After story time for the little ones, they explored the gardens. Elementary students on a field trip searched for answers to questions printed by their teacher. Visitors of all ages enjoyed the park.

The city of Orlando took advantage of the donation of the Gardens in the 1960s to provide a haven for residents to enjoy the botanical garden begun by the Leu family. Small areas of tropical foliage, succulents, native plants, and vegetables greeted us as we meandered along pathways. Butterflies swirled around flora established especially for them.

The collection of specific gardens within the huge park delighted visitors. New vistas came into view along the curved walkways, which encouraged strolling to enjoy the variety of trees, shrubs, and flowers.

When we left the building, the first walkway led to a bubbling stream lined with foliage and shaded by tall trees. A magnificent oak stood by the path. My eyes searched for the top pointing at the azure sky. Gray moss draped its outstretched limbs like a grandparent with welcoming arms for children, grandchildren, and the lonely.

Aged oaks towered over all other trees in the gardens. Their size, longevity, and flaws enhanced their beauty. The weathered, gnarled sentinels had endured a lifetime of storms and struggles. Despite the scars, fractures, and imperfections, they provided safety, shade and a sense of peace.

As members of "Oaks," we also stand tall when anchored in Jesus. Even though scarred, flawed, and imperfect, we welcome with open arms our loved ones and others in need as we provide comfort, deliver love, and offer wisdom.

Loving Father, thank you for guiding, loving, and encouraging us as we face trials. No matter our age, show us how we can love, encourage, and guide those who come behind us.
Amen.

Rebecca Carpenter's roots are in Indiana, but she has called Florida home since her college days. Alongside her late husband, Alan, she embraced a life of adventure that spanned all seven continents—distributing glasses to villagers along the Amazon, walking among penguins in Antarctica, strolling the Great Wall of China, and sharing God's love with students in Namibia. Their journeys to Israel made Scripture come alive in vivid new ways.

Now, Rebecca finds her greatest joy closer to home, tending her beautiful garden (see picture) and seeing God's hand in every bloom, breeze, and sunrise. Her love of creation reflects her deep faith—each plant and creature is a reminder of God's renewal and the quiet hope that grows when we remain rooted in him.

Though her travels have slowed, her spirit of exploration continues as she visits national parks and treasures experiences like the Albuquerque Balloon Festival. Still fueled by wonder and gratitude, she's nearly completed her goal of visiting all fifty states—with only two to go!

Rebecca's passion for writing continues through her son, who shares her love for the written word, and two granddaughters who are following in her literary footsteps. Her life testifies that when we open our hearts to the Holy Spirit, God can still plant new dreams and bring forth fruit—no matter our age or season.

Make sure you follow Rebecca's blog on: http://rebeccacarpenter.blogspot.com.

Also by Rebecca Carpenter

If *Hope in the Garden: 90-Day Devotional* has spoken to your heart, don't miss these other powerful works of encouragement also by Rebecca Carpenter. Both books are available now on Amazon. Simply scan the included QR codes to order your copy today and continue your journey of hope.

HOPE IN ISOLATION: 90-DAY DEVOTIONAL

When life feels lonely or uncertain, this devotional offers daily reminders that you are never truly alone. Each page points you back to God's sustaining presence and His unfailing hope.

In the midst of loss and sorrow, God's glory has a way of breaking through unexpectedly. This heartfelt book brings comfort, healing, and the reminder that beauty can rise even from our deepest grief.

More Publications by Deep Waters Books

For more fine books published by Deep Waters Books
go to www.deepwatersbooks.com or
scan the QR code below: